How to Create a Portfolio & Get Hired

2nd edition

A Guide for Graphic Designers and Illustrators

Fig Taylor

Laurence King Publishing

Author's Acknowledgements

I'd like to thank Liz Resnick for recommending me to write this book, and my commissioning editor, Jo Lightfoot, for having the patience of a saint while I did. I'd also like to thank everyone who gave so generously of their time and experience, enabling me to make a far better job of it than I would have done on my own. In no particular order they are: Bill Finewood, Zoe Antoniou, Jemma Robinson, Alan Male, Andrew Selby, Kim Burdett, Bob Cook, Jane Souyave, Jonathan Gibbs, Nancy Slonims, Phil Gray, Mark Wigan, Steve Wilkin, Will Hill, Al Wasco, Alice Carter, Alisa Aronson, Barbara Yale-Read, Brockett Horne, Deborah Shmerler, Diane Tarter, Edwin Utermohlen, Judith Aronson, Kenenth Fitzgerald, Kimberley Vickrey, Robert Sedlack, Rosario Martinez-Cañaz, Rukmini Ravikumar, Sue Vessella, Tom Garrett, Tyler Galloway, Louisa St Pierre, Ben Cox, Dave Day, Mark Reddy, Neil Dawson, Steve Rutterford, Andy Altman, Andy Ewan, Anne Brassier, Austin Cowdall, Christopher Pullman, Doug Powell, Ian Bilbey, Donough O'Malley, Josh Silverman, Judy Wellfare, Lance Hidy, Danielle Plaskett, Derek Brazell, Martin Lambie-Nairn, Maryanne Grebenstein, Michael Koid, Joshua Keay, Kai Clements, Rian Hughes, Rob Howsam, Robert Linsky, Susan Williamson, Stephanie Zelman, Saeko Ozaki, Stuart Briers, Karen Boller, Alison Lawn, Anamaria Stanley, Colin McHenry, Hazel Brown, Jennifer Pastore, John Oakey, Kristina DiMatteo, Martin Colyer, Paul Harpin, Jim Thompson, Frances McKay, Boo Cook, Kevin Hopgood, Rodd Hunt, Russell Cobb, Steven Preston, Birgitte Lund, Jacqueline Brown, Graham Humphreys, Alex Tomlinson, Anders Suneson, Gert Gerrits, Barry James, Chris Shamwana, Eleanor Crow, Joe Whitlock Blundell, Jonathan Christie, Joy Monkhouse, Lucy Bennett, Mike Jolley, Penny Holroyde, Val Brathwaite, Richard Ogle, Steve Scott, Martin Vintner-Jackson, Neil Lewis, Yuko Shimizu, Jay Taylor, Jeff Fisher, Ulla Puggaard, Andrew Pavitt, Martin Haake, Olaf Hajek, Tina Mansuan, Tomer Hanuka and Siobhan Harrison. If I've left anybody out by mistake, please forgive me!

LAURENCE KING

Laurence King Publishing Ltd
361–373 City Road
London EC1V 1LR
United Kingdom
email: enquiries@laurenceking.com
www.laurenceking.com

A catalogue record for this book is available from the British Library.

ISBN: 978 1 85669 672 2

Senior editor: Zoe Antoniou
Copy editor: Tessa Clark
Picture researcher: Jemma Robinson

Design by Studio Ten and a Half

Printed in China

Contents

Related study material is available
on the Laurence King website at
www.laurenceking.com

Introduction

Designer or illustrator, your chosen industry isn't known as the 'creative jungle' for nothing. And it grows ever denser and more confusing to negotiate as fresh opportunities for visual communicators present themselves. Whoever imagined, even a handful of years ago, that it would be possible to find permanent, well-paid employment designing graphics for mobile phones or avatars for use in cyberspace? Or that collectives of designers and illustrators, and multidisciplinary creative organizations, would become viable, cost-effective alternatives to conventional sources of design and art for some clients? This book is intended to help you make your way through the jungle by understanding the needs of those you're most likely to work for and with – learning what to put inside your new portfolio and, equally importantly, what to leave out, in order to obtain a sought-after position or commission. It's about acknowledging, identifying and focusing on creative employers' often very varied requirements, and meeting them with confidence and professionalism. And it's about accessing and creating job opportunities through a variety of accessible resources.

This is not a book that's overly preoccupied with style. Granted, when addressing the issue of presentation it's impossible to avoid the subject entirely; it is, after all, a designer's or illustrator's job to be stylish, to buck trends and create new ones – and, since your expertise in visual communication is what you are selling, the way your work looks and how you showcase your skills will play a crucial part in determining whether you or another ambitious young newcomer lands the job you are pitching for. So various types of portfolio are represented here along with pointers for putting a presentation together, whether it be physical or virtual. There is also information about promotional material, from websites to printed postcards and other, more unusual leave-behinds. However, I am assuming you know your own mind when it comes to aesthetics. The world is full of coffee-table tomes that wax lyrical about the stylishness of contemporary design and illustration; this is, first and foremost, a book that's concerned with content.

It is also a book about transition: the groundwork you need to lay in order to establish yourself in your chosen career. While most bachelor degree programmes tend to incorporate some information about professional practice, this is noticeably more comprehensive at some art colleges than at others. Attendance at formal, dedicated classes is not always mandatory, and advice may come primarily from visiting lecturers. But even the most valuable information can be ignored unless an individual is genuinely ready to hear it. When you're a student and bursting with great ideas, bringing these to fruition is much more fun than worrying about what you're going to do when you leave college.

Whether you want to be a graphic designer or an illustrator, or perhaps, as is becoming increasingly common in this boundary-blurring digital age, a multi-skilled practitioner, it's a fact that the two disciplines are inextricably linked. It is part of a graphic designer's remit to commission illustrators, if only occasionally; while the illustrator, reliant on those commissions, takes direction from the designer to arrive at the most effective solution for the client footing the bill. At its best, the relationship between designer and illustrator is a partnership, albeit a fleeting one: the coming together of two creative minds trained to solve problems by visual means for commercial purposes – ideally with flair and originality. Like most partnerships, however, it will flounder without clear communication and mutual trust. It's my aim, therefore, to promote understanding and productive relationships between future practitioners – that's why this book addresses aspiring professionals in both camps.

I have had experience of both disciplines: an admittedly short stint as a graphic designer, followed by more than 20 years as an illustrators' agent, working initially with commissioners in design, editorial, publishing, advertising and the gift industry. I also have a concurrent career as portfolio consultant at the Association of Illustrators in London. My work has given me a balanced overview of what employers and commissioners require of graphic designers and illustrators, and insight into the many ways that the marketplace is changing.

This is therefore a book for anyone who is serious about a career in design or illustration, or in the growing number of fields where the two converge. By sharing my experience and that of the many designers and illustrators who have so generously contributed to this book, it's my avowed intention to help you succeed in your chosen sector of the creative industry.

In these pages, you will find not only guidance on how to put together a stunning portfolio that works for you, but also an overview of the range of fields that are open to designers and illustrators today. In addition, quotes from key players in the varying industries are provided throughout, offering soundbites of good advice as well as revealing the range of different opinions you may come across. Along with the wide selection of examples of work, this book is designed to help you along each step of the way.

Some words about language

I'd like to draw your attention to a contentious little adjective that is used in this introduction: 'commercial'. I recall only too well the negative connotations this word had when I was a graphic design student eager to distance myself from my father's professional world, which was advertising. And I meet enough design and illustration students today to realize that little has changed in the interim. So, since I will use the 'C' word during the course of this book, I feel obliged to clear up any misinterpretations from the start.

What I don't mean when I use this potent little epithet is: bland or lacking in artistic merit; creative prostitution, aka selling your soul to the corporate devil; or crass, cynical jumping on to whatever bandwagon happens to be the creative industry's current trend. Nor am I necessarily referring to graphic design or illustrations produced for advertising purposes. Although I'll readily admit that work that falls into all or any of these categories may well be described as commercial, what I mean when I use the term is simply that the work is relevant to the needs of the marketplace at any given time; in other words, if there's a demand for what you're doing within your area of expertise your design or illustration will be deemed (by me at any rate), to be commercial.

Something else I should say on the subject of language is that, since much of the guidance contained in this book applies to both designers and illustrators, I will also use the word 'practitioner' where relevant. The rest of the time references will be subject-specific where appropriate.

What is a Portfolio?

Put simply, a portfolio is a physical or virtual showcase of work. Depending on the stage a designer or illustrator has reached in their development or career, their portfolio may take one or more different forms. There is, however, one constant: because academics and employers have different concerns, the chances are the size, content and format of a practitioner's portfolio will change the most when they make the transition from student to professional. In this chapter you will find the basics on what constitutes the best approach for your portfolio according to your chosen market, to make it an effective tool for your needs.

Opposite (from top, left to right): Three classic examples of how *not* to present work to employers or commissioners; a Pampa Spiral book with polypropylene or polyester sleeves from Prat Paris strikes a more professional note; a Mapac zip-up, ring-bound portfolio with leaves (shown open and closed) is a reliable and smart choice; samples of work, digital and otherwise, can also be accessed online through a PC or Mac, whether transported via a laptop (Acer) or at home and in the studio (Apple Mac Pro).

Opposite: (top) Concept sketches for Loughborough University student Austin Driscoll's Interactive Light Poster; (below) recent University of Northampton graduate Darren Custance's online portfolio.

The Student Portfolio

Initially, regardless of where you choose to study, most art colleges look for similar qualities in the students they enrol. At foundation/undergraduate entry level, interviewing panels want to see a diversity of work including sketchbooks, life-drawing studies and self-initiated endeavours, along with high school projects. Even at this early stage, prospective students who specify an interest in design may be expected to show a flair for the juxtaposition of type and image, while, so far as would-be illustrators are concerned, panels will be on the lookout for strong drawing skills and a keen eye for colour. Experimentation across a wide variety of disciplines, such as painting, photography or printmaking, in both traditional and digital media, is actively encouraged – as is an open mind and a willingness to explore various creative paths. Be aware, though, that there's a distinct difference between showing the range of your work and blindly including everything bar the kitchen sink in your folder on the off chance that somebody, somewhere, might like something. Your ability to discriminate between your best pieces and your less-than-finer efforts will also be under scrutiny, and will continue to be once you graduate, so it's worth starting as you mean to go on.

In terms of how many pieces you should include, it is impossible to be prescriptive; however, using your judgement and making sure you show a wide diversity of work are the best guidelines.

At this stage a portfolio is little more than a receptacle in which to transport work. Given that you'll probably be showing originals, and that some of these will be large, an A1 (24 × 33.9 inch) portfolio, with or without plastic leaves, tends to be the norm. In addition to bearing the hallmark of your creative personality the contents should, where applicable, be mounted up and/or displayed according to individual college guidelines. Some institutions are more prescriptive than others in this respect but meticulously presented samples, put together with obvious pride and in some sort of logical order, always make a favourable impression.

Students wishing to pursue a bachelor degree in graphic design or illustration are expected to demonstrate a distinct leaning towards their chosen subject, but not in so rigid a manner that they come across as 'unteachable' or unwilling to take risks. Whichever discipline you opt to concentrate on, there will be a strong emphasis on the ability to conceptualize and solve problems through image-making – hence the value placed on sketchbooks and developmental roughs. Likewise, projects you've initiated and seen through in your own time will be seen as evidence of commitment and self-motivation.

As a creative practitioner presentations will form a regular part of your working life so, although this is not strictly part of your portfolio, how you write and express yourself verbally can influence your chances of being accepted on a study programme, particularly if the college you choose is a popular one – a factor that is as likely to be influenced by geographical location as by a record of academic excellence. There's every likelihood, too, that you'll be expected to be familiar with leading contemporary practitioners within your field of interest. Aside from anything else it pays to be aware of the competition; and, from an interviewer's perspective, it will prove you're passionate about your chosen discipline and that your decision to study it is an informed one – again, something that will count in your favour if your institution of choice is overwhelmed with applicants.

Those who elect to study for a master's degree have to submit a rather different portfolio – in some ways more akin to the kind they might present to a potential employer or commissioner. The contents are expected to reflect a confidence and sophistication borne of a thorough familiarity with the student's chosen media. However, less is decidedly more at this level, so critical editing skills will once again come into play. The portfolios tend to be significantly smaller in format than the ones produced for initial enrolment in a college and, although the inclusion of sketchbooks and working roughs is equally important, a smaller selection – say 10 or 12 strong, finished pieces – will win out over a larger one that incorporates work you're less sure of. Try to choose the samples that best reflect your unique approach to visual problem-solving or image-making.

Maturity is the key word here; in fact, in the United States (but not in the United Kingdom) it's customary for master's programmes to dictate that students have spent a minimum of a year in the commercial workplace prior to application. Verbal communication skills are of paramount importance. You'll need to be up-to-date with what's under critical debate among industry movers and shakers – and, work experience notwithstanding, your portfolio will have to make clear your ability to undertake sustained, practice-based research. You should also have a clear picture of what you hope to achieve, identifying specific areas of interest you believe would benefit from further development and exploration.

'I would expect to see a set of observational drawings from life; sketchbooks showing the generation and development of ideas as an illustrator; a set of resolved illustrations based on specific texts (with supporting material such as sketchbooks or working sheets). Also some illustration translated into a printed context.'

Jonathan Gibbs, course leader, BA Illustration, Edinburgh College of Art, UK

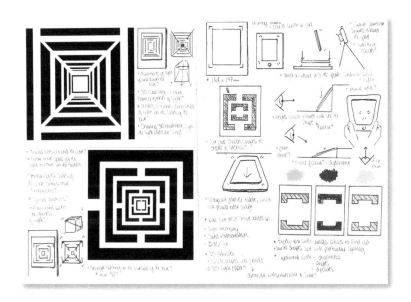

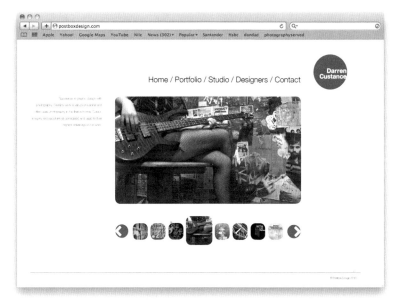

'If a portfolio is totally disorganized and in a real state, I'd worry about the ability of that person to organize themselves and complete a job on time.'

Jonathan Christie, Art Director, Conran Octopus

Below: Digital portfolios can be interactive and allow you to showcase your work on a variety of devices, such as the easily portable iPad. Shown here is work from Tonia Ibrahim's portfolio.

Bottom: Several examples of the box portfolio format, which is particularly effective for prints that need extra attention. These are produced by US company Archival Methods.

B / Create a 'How to ...' Application

C / Apple

M / Multimedia

O / Fully functioning application to be used on an iPad.

Creative block is a common problem. This application helps creatives expand their ideas in a fun and functional way. The illustrative element is friendly to the eye and fun for the user. Featuring photography, typefaces, tutorials, colour swatches, world design, trigger images and design materials.

Overleaf: Darren Custance's online portfolio is bold and simple in keeping with his design aesthetic and ethos. Page 14 features stills from an animation promoting an ePublishing website, while the facing page shows the development and application of a rock band's identity in print and moving image.

The Professional Portfolio

Even if you graduated with flying colours there's inevitably further work to be done on your portfolio if it's to meet with professional requirements. To reiterate, art college lecturers and potential employers have very different agendas when it comes to weighing up the contents of a portfolio. In order to develop your skills and imagination, the college environment will have granted you the freedom to experiment, and your struggles and failures will have played an essential part in discovering where your strengths lie. Those whose job it was to nurture them were concerned primarily with the process of growth, whereas potential employers will be mainly concerned with the finished result. They don't need to see documentary evidence of the mistakes you learnt from. You are, after all, out to inspire confidence not doubt and a patchy portfolio will do the latter. The commercial world is after quality, consistency, focus and enthusiasm – in other words, employability.

Whether you favour a print or digital approach, when it comes to assembling a professional body of work there is no prescribed industry standard, though some colleges offer guidance regarding size, format, number of samples, inclusion of roughs, mounting procedures and so forth. Others merely make recommendations, while many more prefer to leave such decisions to the personal taste of the graduate-to-be. Do bear in mind that large print portfolios are highly impractical, and there is no necessity to show very large pieces at actual size. Presenting on a laptop is an efficient way of transporting large electronic files of work and gives you personal control of your presentation. You can show your work in a small informal meeting or connect the laptop to a projection system and present it in a larger setting. You may prefer to use an interactive tablet device, which, while having a small screen, allows images to be swiftly resized for those wishing to view samples in more detail. A well-organized digital file will enable you to adjust images for multiple formats almost as easily as leafing through the pages of a print portfolio.

The physical aspects of presentation aside, striking a balance between industry requirements and personal expression is vital. College projects can sometimes cramp a nascent practitioner's creative flow in an effort to replicate the rigid budgetary and time constraints of real-life jobs. Conversely, lengthy, deeply personal projects that bear little resemblance to anything a designer or illustrator would be asked to produce in the real world can result in a repetitive or highly uncommercial portfolio. Employers are often willing to make concessions for lack of experience or published work, but a selection of wholly inappropriate samples will baffle, bore and irritate them, and invariably jeopardize your

chances of getting where you want to be.

In order to succeed in a highly competitive market, your portfolio must adequately reflect the needs of your chosen target(s). Unless your degree was highly specialized (for example, in medical illustration), it's likely that, whether you are a designer or an illustrator, you graduated with a little bit of everything in your folder. It will be necessary to decide which of the areas you touched on during the course of your studies interest you the most. You will then need to weed out anything that is no longer relevant and replace it with some fresh work that is.

Several factors could influence the precise contents of your portfolio. If, for instance, you're a designer and are intent on a rural or small town existence, the design companies serving the locale will probably be thin on the ground and therefore more general in nature – ergo, your portfolio must demonstrate adaptability by showing you can apply your skills in a wide variety of contexts. On the other hand, if you are planning to live in a city there'll be far more creative outfits and, consequently, more chance that some of them will be specialist in nature. And speaking of specialization, if you have one in mind – you'd like to be a packaging designer, for example, or a children's book illustrator – you'll need more than a couple of relevant samples to make this perfectly clear.

When it comes to teaching students to promote themselves effectively after they graduate, some art colleges are more up-to-date than others. For instance, given society's increasing reliance on digital technology it is surprising that not all bachelor-degree courses necessarily incorporate building a professional website in their professional studies programmes. As the world grows smaller and employers ever busier, a website is a must. It allows those in other geographical locations and time zones instant access to your work and, for some practitioners, is in effect their portfolio. Even if you choose to go an alternative or more traditional route, your website should be considered an extension of your portfolio and working practice. These methods include your CV, which should be approached as you would any other creative conundrum. You won't convince a much-admired art director of your unparalleled typographic genius with a badly spaced, unspellchecked résumé hastily printed out on photocopy paper. It must be grammatically perfect, typographically matchless and printed out on good-quality stock.

Brief Title: Atelier animation (2)   Concept: The second concept was to have CAD
Brief: To create an animation promoting   illustrations of moving words growing out of a
                    the ebook website   woodland area to connote the transition of the
Media: Screen   new generation of the "book" from the natural

Brief Title:	The Rumor	Concept:	The logo is simplistic and to the point. It says
Brief:	To produce an identity and poster series		who they are; no questions asked. The identity
	for a new rock band The Rumor		features five lines along with a select colour
Media:	Print		pallet within the logo which continues

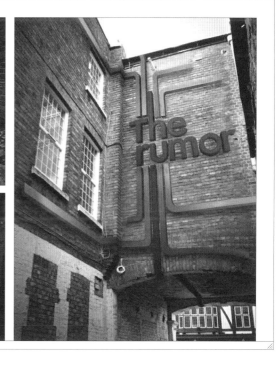

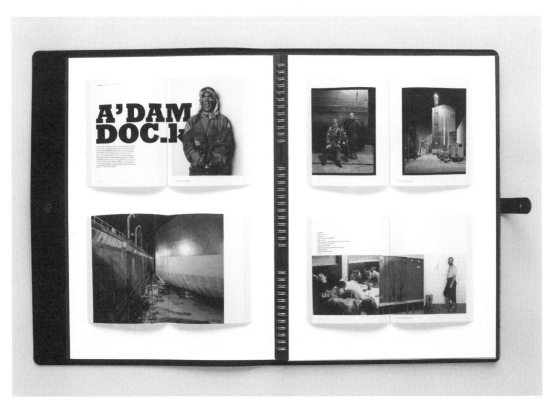

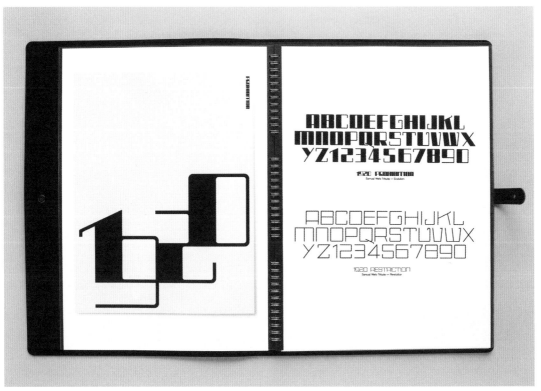

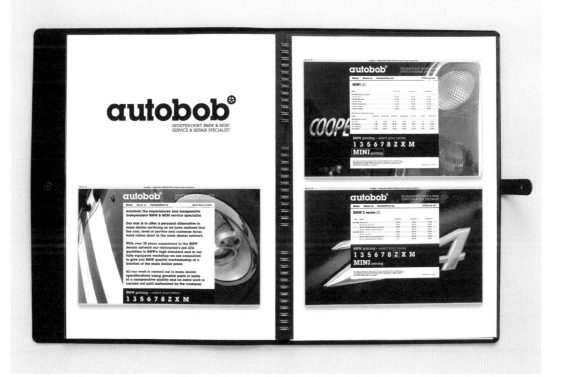

Previous page: Samples from the portfolio
of London-based graphic designer Matt
West whose solo enterprise is called
Two Seventy. As clearly evident from his
portfolio, freelancer Matt works across
a wide variety of disciplines, including
branding, editorial, web and font design.

The Graphic Design Portfolio

A student on the verge of graduation once told me she was torn between a career in advertising and one in magazine design. Unfortunately, she had precisely one advertisement and one magazine spread in her portfolio – so, realistically, she didn't have a hope of landing a job in either. As touched on earlier, if you have ambitions to work in a specific market or discipline, your portfolio needs to reflect this, particularly if your heart is set on full-time employment. A magazine publisher will expect to see a portfolio that shows a sufficient number of spreads; an advertising agency, one crammed with punchy advertising ideas. If your design education was more generalized than specialized you need to research your chosen area thoroughly, then be brutally honest with yourself and decide whether you are genuinely suited to it. (This applies to temperament as well as skills – for instance, if a fast turnover and crazy deadlines aren't for you, you might want to consider a career in book-jacket design rather than one in the frenetic environment of a daily newspaper.) The next step is to put together a dedicated body of work that clearly demonstrates your ambition, and aptitude, to your employer of choice.

'More often than not, a "house style" is a weakness. While personal flavour is fine we are not a "style studio", and have to be able to create a multitude of different technical and stylistic solutions for our clients. Diversity is important.'

Judy Wellfare, Creative Director, Plus et Plus

Even if you are seeking more general and varied work, there are ways to tailor your presentation to a potential employer's needs. Whether you are responding to a job advertisement, or approaching a design outfit on a speculative basis, it is necessary to know something about the ethos of the company and the kind of work they do – otherwise you'll find it difficult to come up with reasons why they should hire you. Finding common ground is an essential part of selling yourself effectively. Do you share the company's unique approach to problem solving or their passion for typography? Are you desperate to work for the kind of clients that hire them? Are you, perhaps, a whizz with the software that is integral to an area of design with which they'd like to be more involved?

Those written and verbal communication skills that got you into art college are equally close to the hearts of potential employers. You need to be able to talk your employer of choice through the conception, development and resolution of each project in your portfolio, identifying how you share their vision, and your relevant skills, along the way; and you will need to be able to do so succinctly.

'In publishing, design for purpose is so important in the sense of applying your style to the various genres – for example, thriller or chick lit – that way of thinking is more important to me than a style.'

Richard Ogle, Art Director, Random House

Attention to detail will impress every bit as much as your redoubtable typographic skills, understanding of composition and ability to conceptualize. Employers will expect you to be suitably qualified technologically, too. (In other words, don't apply for a job as a web designer if you don't know your way around Dreamweaver – unless it is specified that training will be given on the job.) Lastly, versatility, even within a specialist field, is generally viewed as a virtue. Although some employers are impressed by designers who have their own strong, distinguishable 'house style', many consider this a limitation. Clients, on the whole, favour work that is tailored to their needs, so a designer needs to be adaptable, able to translate briefs from a variety of clients in ways suited to their individual needs. For this reason, when applying for a full-time design job it's advisable to include in your portfolio work that shows how far you can take an idea (for example, by applying a logo in many different contexts beyond the usual letterhead and business card). Similarly, be sure to include samples in a variety of media where appropriate. The same advice holds true if you are embarking on a freelance design career: if your portfolio shows that you can design for print, digital and/or interactive media, you'll get more work and a wider variety of it.

Overleaf: Multi-skilled illustrator Andy Smith favours the box portfolio format. For presentation purposes he has one focusing on his typographical work (left) and another on pure illustration (right).

The Illustration Portfolio

Outside the gift industry, computer games developers and the occasional museum, full-time illustration posts are decidedly thin on the ground. Plus, there is no guarantee that even companies that fall into these categories are able to employ in-house illustrators. Most illustrators are therefore freelancers, and for this reason it makes sense for them to appeal to the broadest possible client base.

'I do not have in-house staff to illustrate. It allows me much wider scope to commission the broadest range of illustration rather than be limited to the style of an in-house illustrator/designer. I view illustration as a discipline on its own.'

Alison Lawn, Art Director, *New Scientist*

How you achieve this will largely depend on your geographical location. If you live in a rural district or a locale where there are many more jobs than there are illustrators to do them, having a wide variety of styles in your portfolio will enable you to service more clients. If, however, you live in an area where illustrators vastly outnumber commissions – in a city such as London or New York – you will be infinitely better served by having one (or two, certainly no more than three), distinctive styles in your portfolio and applying these to a wide variety of subjects. Likewise, you can apply different ways of thinking; there is, for instance, no reason why the same illustrative style can't be applied to narrative, decorative, informative and conceptual subject matter.

As a young, London-based illustrators' agent this was something I learnt fast. I was fortunate enough to represent the Australian illustrator Jeff Fisher when he first arrived in the United Kingdom. Australia, vast as it is, has an appreciably smaller illustration industry than Britain. It was clear to me from Jeff's early published work that a highly original style was beginning to evolve, though this applied mainly to commissions where he'd been allowed a free hand. He had also done his fair share of varied bread-and-butter commissions which, had he been London-based from the start, would never have been given to someone with his distinctive illustrative personality. Not realizing that the inclusion of such original work might confuse my clients I immediately set out to dazzle the ones I felt had the most imagination – only to get the response, 'But we

wouldn't know what style we were going to get!' It might have seemed obvious to suggest to them that they simply point to the style they liked, but they were spoilt for choice so why should they take the risk of ending up with a different one?

The more well served the market, the pickier clients can afford to be. Showing too many styles to a fussy client introduces the career-cramping element of doubt; it makes the illustrator look capricious and unreliable instead of steady and dependable. Unless you are sidestepping into the textile or gift industries, where constant stylistic reinvention is a necessity, it's better to commit yourself to what you know you do best than try to be all things to all clients. Meanwhile, those multi-talented individuals who suffer from creative restlessness and find it genuinely impossible to commit to a signature style, may need to put together more than one portfolio, each geared towards a different type of commissioner, in order to market themselves efficiently.

'All I really look for is an individual voice, a strong sense of design (composition I suppose), and something intangible that makes me think I could never produce that image myself. Logistics of delivery and deadlines can always be solved, but a great image is never just a matter of problem solving.'

Jonathan Christie, Art Director, Conran Octopus

The Cross-disciplinary Portfolio

At the risk of stating the obvious, being a cross-disciplinary practitioner is not the same as having 25 illustrative styles or designing for print and virtual media. It's embracing more than one discipline – the graphic designer/photographer who exhibits in galleries and runs their own clothing label on the side or the illustrator who art directs and/or animates. If you fall into this category you'll find that commissioners and employers are as likely to be confused by you as they are to welcome you with open arms. So, once again, pre-presentation research is a must and will probably dictate the bias, or order, of the work you show at an interview.

'[A cross-disciplinary approach] shows flexibility. Airside work across all media so we like designers who can too.'

Anne Brassier, PR and New Business, Airside

Some employers are more visionary or broad-minded than others. There are design consultancies, for instance, that will happily engage a full-timer on the basis that he or she has a couple more strings to their bow. Conversely, others will take a more rigid approach when hiring staff, preferring to engage the services of freelance specialists when necessary. Similarly, some book-cover designers love nothing more than a type-savvy illustrator; whereas an editorial art director with a team of in-house layout designers might find a design-heavy element in what they've been led to believe is an illustrator's portfolio irrelevant or off-putting. Curiously, when I questioned one editorial art director about this matter he expressed a marked preference for specialist practitioners when hiring full-time design staff, but great enthusiasm for cross-disciplinary portfolios when commissioning illustrators.

Up until relatively recently multi-skilled designers probably stood the best chance of utilizing all their talents as freelancers, but the industry is changing and new ways of working are beginning to appear. Those who work across a variety of disciplines are starting to collaborate with people of like mind, pooling their resources to form collectives and hybrid creative consultancies. Artists previously thought of as cultish have emerged from the underground and into the mainstream. Graphic novelists, graffiti artists, creators of hip vinyl toys, computer games developers, embellishers of designer skateboards and designers whose graphics have become synonymous with club culture have tremendous appeal to clients keen to connect with the youth demographic. Indeed, the most adventurous of them are starting to bypass conventional agencies, preferring to approach artists and collectives directly in the hope of getting something fresher. Illustration agencies, too, are starting to represent cross-disciplinary practitioners and collaborators in response to clients who want to use their artists in less traditional ways.

'It depends on many factors: how the work is presented, the sophistication of the designer (are they able to rationalize the decision for presenting a cross-disciplinary body of work? Are they able to tie the various areas together in a cohesive whole?). I think most young designers can improve their marketability by having a broad set of skills – assuming it is not watered down.'

Doug Powell, Creative Director, Schwartz Powell Design

It is therefore not surprising that, where presentation is concerned, there are as yet no hard and fast rules for the multi-skilled. However, given the increasing complexity of the marketplace and the rapidity with which it is changing, you will almost certainly need to be flexible. Creating more than one portfolio may be the simplest option – or dividing the one you have into different sections dedicated to the various facets of your creative personality. A lot will depend on how open-minded your target is likely to be, and the nature of the work you are hoping to get from them. If in doubt it's always good to ask.

Summary
What is a Portfolio?

1.

A portfolio showcases work and takes on different forms depending on the stage a designer or illustrator has reached in their development or career.

2.

An entry-level student portfolio shows the interviewing panel at the applicant's chosen art college the diversity of their work, and should reflect an ability to create concepts and solve problems through image-making. A portfolio submitted for a master's degree is more sophisticated, and is similar to one that might be used in a presentation to a potential employer or client.

3.

A professional portfolio must strike a balance between personal expression and the needs of the creative industry. A website should be seen as an extension of your portfolio.

4.

A graphic design portfolio needs to be tailored to a potential employer's requirements, and should clearly demonstrate the designer's abilities and aptitude.

5.

An illustration portfolio has to appeal to a broad client base, as most illustrators are freelance. Although showing a wide variety of styles makes sense where there is relatively little competition, illustrators in more competitive environments should develop a strong, recognizable style and apply it to a diverse range of subject matter.

6.

A cross-disciplinary portfolio appeals to more visionary and broad-minded clients, and those who want to connect with the youth demographic. Multi-skilled practitioners need to be flexible when it comes to deciding what samples to show, and it may be necessary to create more than one portfolio.

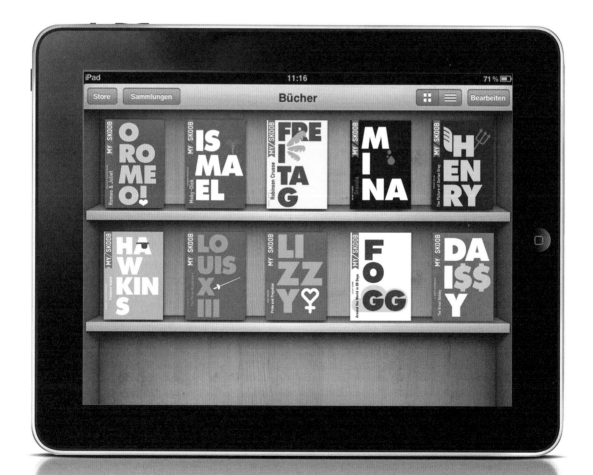

Making Sense of the Marketplace

2

Familiarizing yourself with the various sectors in the creative marketplace is the first step to deciding who to approach for work. You need to know about the key areas in the industry, the positions that are available in each one, how the commissioning process works in different sectors and, before you start to create your portfolio, the design or illustration skills required by potential employers or clients. All this tends to be something practitioners learn over time – sometimes to their personal cost or too late in the day. This chapter aims to help you embark on the most suitable path from the outset.

Opposite: eBooks for download onto PC, tablet, mobile phone or eReader offer exciting opportunities for those wishing to explore the ever-expanding area of interactive design. MySkoob is an ePublisher offering classic literature in an enhanced digital format via an innovative blend of bold, graphic type, illustration and photography. The result is the brainchild of award winning German design agency, Strichpunkt, who are responsible for MySkoob's branding across a variety of media. The books are also available in equally dynamic print form, quaintly described as offline eBooks.

'Were I hiring an entry-level designer,
it would certainly be to their advantage to
have had some experience in a professional
design environment – but not mandatory.'

Doug Powell, Creative Director, Schwartz Powell Design

Below: As well as the packaging of comestibles, music also forms part of the packaging designer's remit, either as an individual object or part of a bigger branding project. This design, as well as the logotype, was created by Non-Format for the Lo Recordings 2007 release, *Jean-Jacques Perrey and Luke Vibert Present Moog Acid*. The striking font compliments the miniature models and photography by Dan McPharlin.

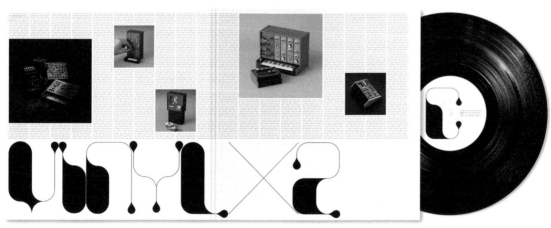

Design Groups

Design groups differ in many ways. They can range from tiny two-person partnerships that hire freelance help as and when necessary, through to large organizations with full-time employees and offices around the world. They can also vary in terms of the kinds of service they offer and, accordingly, the practitioners they employ – for instance, some favour a strictly typographic approach while others are avowedly pro-illustration. Some companies are broad-based and/or multidisciplinary, while others concentrate their creative energies on certain types of client, such as the entertainment or fashion industry, the corporate/financial sector, or disciplines such as typographical or web design. Areas of specialization frequently overlap and include: branding and corporate identity; marketing communications; company reports; packaging and product design; publishing; exhibition design; and design for the web and other digital media. Although many companies concentrate on the last, design for print still predominates. Stationery, brochures, catalogues, handbooks, menus, price lists, prospectuses, customer magazines, direct mail, point-of-sale material, and so forth, all fall within this category, as does the packaging of food and drink, beauty products, CDs, DVDs and other luxuries and necessities.

The digital realm – the medium that has led to ever more diversity where design is concerned – is your salvation. It is difficult to find a design group without a website, so get online, and check out client lists and staff profiles as well as the kind of skills potential employers want to see in a portfolio.

Branding

Companies that specialize in branding offer their clients development and growth strategies borne from intensive market research in addition to design services – while the design services they offer frequently extend beyond the graphic. The organizations that most commonly refer to branding consultants include those in the food and beverage market; the fashion, retail, sports and entertainment industries; the mass media; and the voluntary sector. A branding project could range from providing a simple logo for a fledgling business to formulating and implementing a company's entire ethos. Depending on the type of client, the nature of the job, and the media involved a branding consultancy might bring in freelancers from areas other than graphic design or illustration, such as product and industrial designers, film-makers, interior designers or architects. Adaptability and the ability to be a team player are therefore a must for practitioners considering a branding career, as are

enthusiasm for research and a passion for popular visual culture. It's also worth mentioning that some large corporations, most notably those involved in retail, entertainment and fashion, have their own in-house design departments and/or branding teams.

'An all-rounder and team player is the one who will find it easiest to survive and thrive… This designer is one who is not hampered by 2-D or 3-D, is as at home online as in print or in the built form. Do enough research on brands you admire and, working backwards, find out who worked on them creatively. Call them up and ask them for work experience. You will almost never see an advertisement for a "brand designer". It's not a job; it's a business-support sector.'

Susan Williamson, Retail Consultant, The Chambers

'We are a small company and we have to have people that can multitask, and people that are not beyond tea-making, as well as having the confidence to sit in meetings and voice their ideas. We do nurture though; they get lots of constructive feedback.'

Anne Brassier, PR and New Business, Airside

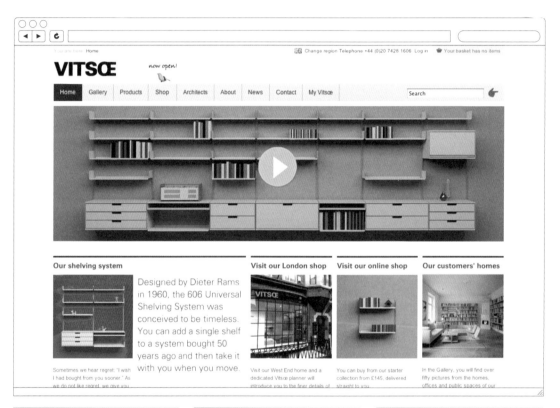

Opposite: When European shelving company Vitsœ's text-heavy website began to feel dated, Airside designed one to attract a new, global generation of customers. The clean, uncluttered result admirably reflects Vitsœ's ethos of 'less but better' and features a new catalogue of photographs and videos (top). The frames (bottom) are taken from a two-minute animation telling the story of Vitsœ's 606 storage system.

Below: Airside's own website features a shop, allowing their multidisciplinary team an outlet for more personal creative projects. Anne Brassier's unique knitted critters (she claims to have found them behind her tool shed), the Stitches, are collector's items. Some, once 'adopted', even go on to start their own blogs!

Design for digital media

The Internet is a rapidly expanding and constantly evolving area, and a digitally-oriented design company is likely to employ designers to maintain its own online presence, as well as to create websites, microsites, banners, icons, flash animations or apps for its clients. Similarly, all manner of businesses employ staff to design and manage their websites – so practising as a website designer may not always involve working in a strictly creative environment. Although some digital design companies offer a degree of training on the job, most entry-level designers are expected to have a working knowledge of various software applications (most commonly Adobe Illustrator, Photoshop, Dreamweaver and/or Flash), and codes (specifically HTML, DHTML, XHTML and CSS). Code is particularly important. As the boundary between designer and developer becomes increasingly blurred with technological advancement, it helps if you speak the same language. Web designers who want a freelance career should bear in mind that full-timers tend to have more simply defined roles and fewer responsibilities, as dedicated back-up staff are usually employed to deal with the everyday maintenance and administration that keep a site up and running. Time spent liaising with clients, uploading new content, and updating and amending existing information can seriously reduce the amount of time available for designing.

Multidisciplinary design

Broad-based organizations are generally appreciative of designers who can work across several disciplines. This applies especially to smaller ones where budgets are tight, resources are pooled and everyone is expected to pull their weight. Ditto those with little in the way of competition; a design group based in a rural area is likely to service an appreciably wider variety of clients than a niche consultancy in a thriving big city – and will require its designers to have a broader repertoire in order to accommodate the needs of diverse clients. A graphic designer's illustrative or photographic skills might be used if their work is suitable for a project. However, larger companies used to working with high-profile clients, or organizations with significantly higher budgets, may prefer their designers to concentrate solely on design. All groups work differently and there's no way of knowing what their requirements are unless these are specified in a job advertisement – or unless you ask. So ask.

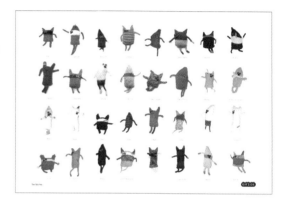

'TV and print are only two facets of what we produce now. We are operating on all interactive and digital platforms. All teams participate not only on all known aspects of traditional advertising but also inventing apps, creating installations, websites, events, virals, etc. BBH now has a digital department called 'Addictive Pixel'

Mark Reddy, Head of Art, BBH London

'Most designers coming out of college know
a little basic coding. Our main skill here is the
story telling for brands which can be told over
multiple platforms. We always make sure the
look and feel of the design is nailed first before
it's coded.'

Stephen Rutterford, Owner, The Brooklyn Brothers, New York

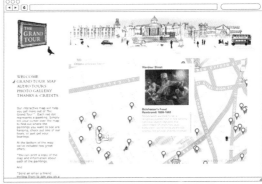

Opposite: While print is still in demand, digital technology has added fresh dimensions to graphic design. The Grand Tour was a public art project in which framed reproductions of National Gallery artworks were hung in London streets (top). Interactive communications agency, Digit, were hired to create a series of multi-information feeds designed for mobile phones, MP3 players and the web. In addition to photographs, the website (bottom) included downloadable maps of the artworks' locations, and themed tours that could be downloaded as podcasts or printouts.

Below: Brooklyn's Studio NewWork produce a biannual, large-format arts publication, showcasing the work of a wide range of visual artists and creative thinkers in all spheres. It also serves to highlight NewWork's innovative approach to design, featuring bold, custom-designed typefaces and removable layouts that also function as posters.

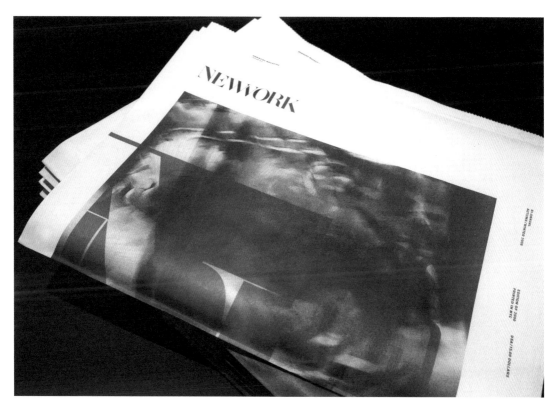

Below: Non-Format is the creative direction and design team of Kjell Ekhorn and Jon Forss, whose wide-ranging work encompasses branding and packaging to publishing and advertising. Their illustrative skills are here expressed in their advertisement for *The Economist* magazine, whose subject of focus was 'balance'.

Opposite: D&AD is a British educational charity, which exists to promote excellence in design and advertising, culminating in an annual Awards show. UK illustration collective, Le Gun, were commissioned to produce life-size illustrations by Studio8 Design, who also themed and designed the promotional material for the event, which took place at London's Royal Festival Hall in 2008.

Design internships

For designers, a design internship can pave the way to a full-time job and some design groups only hire juniors who have done a placement with the company. However, it is worth noting that a permanent job is not necessarily given, nor are all graduate internships paid beyond travel expenses, particularly in the current economic climate. The majority of student placements are also largely unpaid as they are generally viewed as a continuation of the education process. Familiarize yourself with what various groups do and approach one that interests you with a view to arranging a work placement. If you're lucky, you may land one of the few paid internships that are very occasionally advertised. Overall, advertisements for inexperienced junior designers are few and far between, but they do sometimes appear in industry magazines, national and regional newspapers, creative recruitment websites, and design groups' individual websites, many of which state an interest in seeing work by new designers. Make a point of visiting as many sites as possible and get used to making speculative overtures.

Illustration commissions

It is not recommended for illustrators to approach a design company before they have published work – usually commissioned in the editorial sector, as discussed later in this chapter – to show in their portfolio. The bigger the budget, the more parties involved in the development of a job, and the less creatively inclined the client who is paying for the work, the more likely it is that an organization will need to see published, relevant work. So, once you have carved a niche for yourself in business and financial journals, for instance, try contacting design groups that service the same type of publication. Your work will be familiar to the decision-makers in these areas and will therefore appeal to clients who are targeting this kind of audience. Similarly, if you have provided decorative solutions for food and drink magazines you'll be in with a chance with any company that specializes in packaging for this sector.

To look for leads to the kinds of art different design companies are looking for, comb design magazines and blogs for updates on what they are up to.

'I've had a few awkward encounters in the past with people who refuse to change their "art". I've had some who just don't get the concept however many times you explain it... The artists who are the most successful are talented but, more importantly, professional.'

Steve Rutterford, Art Director, Brooklyn Brothers

'I pick a simple project to engage an intern,
who, in turn, becomes a junior designer, and
then as they prove themselves along the way,
assign them more responsibilities.'

Josh Silverman, President/Founder/Minister of Perspective, Schwadesign, Inc.

Below: Designer Ed Watt devised the visual identity and advertising for 'Kick-Out Bigotry', Scottish football's united campaign against religious discrimination. Aimed at fans, officials, clubs and authorities, this campaign, on behalf of charity Football For All, appeared in various formats around major stadium locations. Shown here (from top, left to right) are the typeface, football, beer mats and one of a series of escalator panels placed throughout the Glasgow underground system.

Advertising Agencies

Advertising is not a metier for the faint-hearted. Designer or illustrator, you need to have your wits about you and be prepared to work extremely hard – late nights, all-nighters, even weekends on occasion, if that's what it takes – though, in most cases, you will be handsomely remunerated. There is a lot of money in this sector. Advertising space doesn't come cheap and neither does advertising creativity, especially where blue chip accounts are concerned.

A commercial can take several forms: print advertisements can appear on poster sites, as direct mail or in the press, while moving image ads can be aired on TV, in movie theatres, or released virally on the internet. In common with design companies, many ad agencies are involved with digital media, using apps, games, websites and the like to communicate with their clients' target audiences. Since there are a wide variety of platforms, tools and technologies used to support interactive programming, an awareness of the potential of using these is an absolute necessity. A campaign – generally a minimum of three consecutive advertisements – can be local, national or global, and might use a single medium or a combination of media to get its point across. Given that each of these requires a slightly different approach, some agencies – such as those who concentrate on direct mail – elect to specialize in certain mediums. Others take a more broad-based approach, though they may target specific sectors, such as pharmaceuticals or the motor industry. Research will be necessary to identify which agencies are most likely to be interested in your work and which of them will grant you an interview.

'I search online or ask a friend about illustrators, but I'm constantly looking and keep a mental note of things I like. When a relevant job comes up I remember that illustrator/photographer and take it from there.'

Dave Day, Art Director, Fallon

Routes into advertising design

Getting into advertising as a designer, even if you did a specialized degree and/or come ready-partnered with your own copywriter, is no cakewalk. You'll need to be determined, resilient and gregarious, as networking is about the only way to get a foot in the door. There are some resources to help you: professional organizations and educational charities such as Design and Art Direction (D&AD) and Young Creative Network (YCN) in the United Kingdom, and the Art Directors Club, the One Club and AIGA (the professional association of design) in the United States, are committed to nurturing and showcasing emerging talent, and provide opportunities to connect with industry professionals. Glance at any agency website, however, and you'll see no mention of jobs for entry-level designers; you're also unlikely to see any advertisements in newspapers or on recruitment sites for junior designers, barring ones that specify a year or two's professional experience.

The general route into advertising at a junior level is via work placements. These can last anything from a fortnight to three or four months and, unlike those in other sectors, tend to be offered to graduates rather than students. The longer your stay the better, as there is more time to demonstrate your talent in addition to your teamworking and time-management skills, which are essential to the job. An ambitious design intern with clear potential might be offered a full-time position following a placement, but many designers embark on a series of internships, after which they should have built up a CV that will interest headhunters, and made sufficient contacts to be privy to the advertising industry grapevine. Needless to say, the more well-respected the agencies you secure placements with, the more employable you will ultimately become (and the less likely it is that you'll be exploited while you are working your way up). Blue chip clients paying high fees demand the best, so the more prestigious the agency, the more picky it is when it is hiring a newcomer.

In theory, a larger agency has some leeway for nurturing, while a smaller one can provide more one-on-one time with senior creatives. Some operate placement schemes that students can apply for during their final year of college. These are largely promoted through professional organizations such as the ones mentioned above, or on the agencies' own websites. However, many more internships come about informally following a speculative pitch. Given that your chosen career involves dreaming up innovative ways to sell products, selling yourself shouldn't present too much of a problem. (If it does, you'd best quit now while you're still ahead.) You can make your pitch as a solo practitioner, but you usually need to have a copywriting partner; however, since aspiring copywriters also make overtures to agencies, and the custom is to work in a creative duo, the agency can partner you up when you get there.

The creative director is the person to target with promotional

Below: Direct mail is a form of
advertising sometimes handled by design
and/or branding consultancies. Shown
here is part of a direct mail package
designed by Nic Shuttleworth for creative
marketing agency Iris Associates for Voice,
a telemarketing service for whom Iris came
up with the name, brand identity and
business strategy.

material. Some of them loathe gimmicks while others are more
kindly disposed, but the general consensus is that if you decide
to go the gimmicky route, you must do something amazing. It's
a fine line to tread. The young hopeful who submitted a portfolio
that contained raw fish and the message 'Do you have a plaice
for us?' obviously hadn't anticipated its contents decomposing.
It took some time for the agency staff to locate the as yet
unviewed portfolio as the source of the smell, which lingered
for months. On the other hand, one aspiring young team wrote
to the head of the same creative department in the guise of a
lady who claimed to have enjoyed a brief dalliance with him
some 22 years previously. 'She' revealed that, as a consequence,
she'd borne nonidentical twin boys who now wanted to work
in advertising – and, having brought them up alone and seen
them through art college, she fondly hoped he'd do the decent
thing by them. Happily, the team's audacity paid off. They
ended up working for the agency for some years and, when
they finally left for pastures new, their 'mother' wrote to thank
the creative director for looking after his boys.

Once you've engaged a potential employer's attention,
it goes without saying your portfolio should predominantly
contain advertisements, preferably in a format that's direct and
easy to digest in a short time. If television commercials are your
thing, storyboards, or 'scamps', are preferable to lengthy show
reels. Interruptions happen frequently in a high-pressure
environment and you can't take the risk of losing your
interviewer's attention.

'You can't come into this business and
be precious because your work dies
all the time.'

Neil Dawson, Global Creative Director, Philips, DDB

Routes into advertising illustration

Illustrators can target individual art directors but the best route is usually via an art buyer. Buyers are formidable individuals with tough hides, colourful vocabularies and memories like Rolodexes. A big agency might employ three or four of them, some of whom may be more interested in illustration than others, so try to find out who you should contact before making an approach. A buyer's role is essentially to keep track of the resources creatives need: illustrators, photographers, stylists, model agencies and so forth. They also negotiate fees and tend, for the most part, to be on the side of the artist. A good one will be well acquainted with the agency's creative teams and the accounts they are working on, and will therefore know who is looking out for what. What's more, they'll have no compunction about physically hauling a creative out of their office to look at a portfolio there and then.

There is always the possibility that an advertising agency might approach you, depending, of course, on the extent to which your illustrations have been published: the more work you have in annuals, on websites and in print the more likely it is to be noticed. Should this happen, do your research into the agency before your presentation, and try to include published samples you feel are relevant to its clients.

> **'Seeing new fresh work can inspire me to create a campaign based around their work.'**
>
> Steve Rutterford, Art Director, Brooklyn Brothers

If your work is so far unpublished, my advice is to wait until you are reasonably established before contacting an agency, especially if it's a big one. Although many creatives enjoy discovering and working with fresh illustration talent, the decision as to whether a particular artist is right for a job doesn't ultimately rest with them. A junior creative has to convince his superiors, who in turn have to convince the account handler, whose job it is to sell the illustrator's work to the client who hired the agency. A company can spend millions on a campaign, so it wants to be very sure that an illustrator can do the job. If it agrees to using one who can't, it will have to pay him/her a substantial rejection fee; and the agency will have to find a replacement illustrator to do the job properly, in five seconds flat – yesterday. Examples of work in a portfolio that are relevant can help!

Not all illustrators are suited to working in advertising, and having a fashionable style is only one part of the equation. Because of the number of people involved, and the various vetting stages before a job can finally go ahead, deadlines can shrink from weeks to days, tempers become short and demands seem highly unreasonable. In addition, advertising briefs can be tight and prescriptive, leaving little room for self-expression. But some adrenalin junkies do their best work under pressure, and the financial rewards can be great. The more media used to convey the advertiser's message, the wider the geographical area the campaign covers and the longer it runs, the fatter the final fee will be. Some illustrators find it helpful to regard advertising commissions as a means to subsidize lower-paid jobs that allow more creative freedom.

Opportunities for cross-disciplinary practitioners

Although creative directors are keen to commission freelance cross-disciplinary practitioners, traditional agencies are not generally interested in offering them full-time work. Creatives in advertising are primarily employed as art directors, and for their thinking skills, and agencies are wary of jacks-of-all-trades – any additional skills a designer or illustrator can offer are definitely viewed as optional extras. Exceptions to this rule are very small agencies or start-ups, where multiple roles are born of necessity. Less traditional creative consultancies, and collectives that pride themselves on being multidisciplinary, are also likely to offer more scope to practitioners who wish to bring a variety of skills to the table.

Below: Advertising has many outlets. This outdoor poster campaign (top) by designer/illustrator Erica Jacobson was produced for Nordic directory enquiries service, Eniro. Integrated agency Exposure's 'Friends of British Summertime' campaign (bottom) ran across various media, including radio, press and the web to boost brand awareness of cider manufacturer, Bulmers.

Opposite: Spanish illustrator Adrià Fruitós created all the characters and artwork used to promote theatre company Dagoll Dagom's 2007–8 production of *Boscos Endins* (Into The Woods). His work featured in a dedicated website as well as advertising posters and other printed promotional material (right); and he also created a mural inside the theatre (bottom left).

Below: The editorial arena extends far beyond well-known consumer titles. *Gulf Life* (produced by Ink Publishing) is the in-flight magazine for Middle Eastern airline, Gulf Air, and falls into the category of the customer (also called custom) magazine. Certain publishing houses specialize in titles aimed at the customers, employees and clients of large companies and organizations.

Opposite: The *Radio Times* is the UK's premium listings magazine for all major terrestrial, cable and satellite television channels, as well as all radio stations. The *Doctor Who* spread (bottom) typifies the magazine's strong visual style and in-depth articles. The four covers (top), illustrated by Kris Kasch, were commissioned to celebrate the BBC documentary *The Seven Ages of Rock*. They were designed as four collectables, that when put together, make one complete image.

The Editorial Sector

Editorial is a wide-ranging area that takes in everything from daily newspapers to weekly magazines and newspaper supplements, and monthly and quarterly 'glossy' publications; it also includes trade and professional publications, freebies and consumer magazines. In addition to traditional print format, these may be made accessible online or produced for digital download on tablet, mobile phone or eReader.

Openings for designers

Some magazine publishers have the kind of structure that enables them to hire designers (both print- and web-based) fresh out of college and take the requisite time to nurture and mentor them. Others stipulate that applicants for junior design positions must already have some industry experience. This can vary from a fortnight – easy enough to arrange as a college placement – to a year, which obviously presents more of a challenge.

Internships can often lead to full-time employment; indeed, some magazines prefer to fill junior design positions this way and never advertise them. However, since you'll be hard-pressed to find an internship that lasts more than a few months, try to arrange as much editorial work experience as you can (do note, however, that college internships are generally unpaid and, such is the stiff competition in this area, some graduates are prepared to hustle for an unpaid internship simply for the experience). In the mean time, Your college might offer you work on live editorial briefs, but you could also volunteer your design skills to a local school or charity. Paid or unpaid, if it's in print and shows what you can do, it will count in your portfolio. Learn, too, to capitalize on any connections you make in the editorial sector. Keep in touch with anyone who expresses an interest in your work. If a magazine is short-staffed due to sickness, injury or maternity leave the art editor might be desperate enough to ask the promising, if inexperienced, young designer they saw last month to help out for a day or two. (This is exactly how I came by my first professional engagement, after initially being told to come back in a year by the design company in question. I was the last graduate they'd seen, and therefore the first they remembered when the art director's assistant took off on a spur-of-the-moment three-week holiday.)

It's important to give serious thought, sooner rather than later, to the type of magazine for which your design abilities are best suited. Working on a publication with a less-is-more aesthetic requires a different sort of eye – to say nothing of a different set of technical skills – to working on one crammed

with images and bite-size features. Snobbery abounds in the editorial arena; the choices you make at the start of your career can have a significant impact on its future path, and designers can find themselves typecast. It's worth bearing in mind that the magazine you choose to read may not necessarily be the kind of publication you will enjoy designing.

'**The nature of our business with tight deadlines and a lot of products means that most designers have to learn pretty quickly, but there are senior staff on hand to help throughout the learning process to ensure deadlines are met… If a graduate shows creative flair and technical ability the lack of experience could be overlooked.**'

John Oakey, Art Director, *TimeOut* Group

Both magazine and newspaper design require the ability to work to grids and style sheets, a good eye and a thorough working knowledge of QuarkXPress, InDesign and Photoshop. However, newspaper design offers less scope for creativity as turnover is fast, deadlines short and the environment more pressurized, particularly for daily newspapers. Many magazines, when interviewing designers, will require them to design a sample spread in order to gauge how well they understand the design aesthetic of the publication.

'It's always worth running new developments in your work past art editors. A couple of illustrators I have seen have done this, and I have often liked their new direction more and have commissioned them on the back of that.'

Hazel Brown, Deputy Art Editor, *Radio Times*

Overleaf: the increasing use of tablets, eReaders and other handheld devices has increased the demand for eMagazines and apps. UK industry bible, Design Week, originally began life in print in the early 1990s. Now entirely web-based, it is currently free to access, along with its extensive archive.

As easy as
⌘P.

SIGN UP FOR NEWS ALERT

ADVERTISE

CONTACT US

Sunday, 22 April 2012

SEARCH

Sign In | Register | Advanced search

HOME   NEWS   WE LIKE   VOXPOP   BRANDING   GRAPHICS   INTERACTIVE   PRODUCT   DIRECTORY   AWARDS   JOBS

BRANDING

EDITORIAL

EXHIBITION

FURNITURE

GRAPHICS

INTERACTIVE

INTERIORS

PACKAGING

PRINT

NEWS

WE LIKE

Make your own robots 🖨
Fri, 20 Apr 2012

This kit features robot designs from David Shrigley, Airside and

LATEST JOBS

SENIOR INTERIOR DESIGNER STUDIO INDIGO

JUNIOR / MID DESIGNER ODYSSEY 2011

MIDDLE WEIGHT INTERIOR ARCHITECT/TECHNICIAN

PRODUCT

RETAIL

Design Week on Twitter

dw Design_Week
Powell Allen
has created this
maze–like
identity for a
youth
organisation:
bit.ly/HYu8Ux
yesterday · reply ·
retweet · favorite

twitter Join the
conversation

dw Design
Week on
Facebook

👍 Like   435

FOLLOW ME ON Pinterest

RSS FEEDS

This year's D&AD Yellow Pencil winners in design
Fri, 20 Apr 2012

A round-up of the the 2012 design Yellow Pencil winning projects.

Powell Allen's maze-like identity

others.

MORE

VOXPOP

What is the best use of a QR code that you have seen?
Thu, 19 Apr 2012

Steve Osborne's recent article looked at the use if technologies such as QR code on packaging. What is the best use of a QR code that you have seen?

Which gameshow would you like to redesign?
Fri, 13 Apr 2012

The Apprentice? The Generation Game? Funhouse...?

Which album cover would you like to update?
Thu, 5 Apr 2012

Sir Peter Blake updated his Sgt Pepper designs - which album would you change?

MORE

STUDIO INDIGO

SENIOR DESIGNER, GLOBAL MARKETING COMMUNICATIONS PRIME FOCUS

WEB DESIGNER VITABIOTICS

If only we could bill more time.

for Transform Coaching

Fri, 20 Apr 2012

The branding for this youth organisation represents 'the journey of transformation'

The Team and Cisco develop virtual mirrors for John Lewis

Fri, 20 Apr 2012

The Team and Cisco have developed two virtual fashion mirrors for retailer John Lewis' flagship store on Oxford Street.

MORE

London Film Museum to open Covent Garden outpost

Fri, 20 Apr 2012

Brand Nu and KPF have worked on designs for a new exhibition space.

My Feelings Like You

Fri, 20 Apr 2012

Gary Taxali's Pop-influenced work - playful, pretty and poignant.

streamtime

MOST POPULAR	MOST COMMENTED	MOST EMAILED

HEINZ LAUNCHES VINTAGE LABELS FOR DIAMOND JUBILEE

THIS YEAR'S D&AD YELLOW PENCIL WINNERS IN DESIGN

WHAT IS THE BEST USE OF A QR CODE THAT YOU HAVE SEEN?

PETER AND PAUL DESIGNS CREATIVE ENGLAND IDENTITY

THE REFRESHED DESIGN WEEK WEBSITE

LATEST OPPORTUNITIES

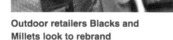

The anatomy of a Honda Civic

Thu, 19 Apr 2012

Artist Ryoji Ikeda has created an AV installation using the raw CAD data used to design the Honda Civic car.

Outdoor retailers Blacks and Millets look to rebrand

Mon, 2 Apr 2012

Blacks Leisure Group is understood to be looking to rebrand its Blacks and Millets brands.

University of Gloucestershire seeks graphics consultancy

Thu, 15 Mar 2012

The University of Gloucestershire is seeking to appoint a graphic design consultancy.

MORE

2012 James Dyson Award open for entries

Fri, 3 Feb 2012

The James Dyson Award challenges youg designers and engineers to develop problem-solving inventions.

The London Original Print Fair

Wed, 18 Apr 2012

Work from Peter Blake, David Hockney, Tracey Emin and others will go on show.

MORE

ANALYSIS

Below: 'Snob Magazine' is aimed at successful Russian-speaking professionals around the world, and features stories on a range of topics designed to appeal to the intelligent reader. Illustration is prevalent in the publication, from the covers by staff designer Alexandra Kuznetsova (top centre) and illustrator/musician Key Wilde (top right), to spreads (bottom) by New York-based British illustrator Peter Arkle. Art direction is by Ilya Baranov.

Opposite: *Utne Reader* (top) is a bi-monthly digest publication bringing together the best of the alternative and independent press to a clued-up, forward thinking readership. Shown here is a spread from *Blue Notes*, illustrated by Nate Johannes and art directed by Stephanie Glaros (Nov/Dec 2008). The Australian bi-monthly magazine *frankie* (bottom) also predominantly uses illustration, as shown here by artist Sara Hingle.

Blue Notes

The life-giving link between mood and musical expression
by Moira Farr, from the Walrus ✳ Illustrations by Nate Johannes

I've never met Garnet Rogers. For all I know, he's a very nice man. Like his late brother, Stan, he sure can sing. But 10 years ago, Garnet nearly killed me at the Canadian Tulip Festival in Ottawa, and I've wondered ever since whether certain musicians shouldn't issue statements at the beginning of their concerts. "Warning: This performance contains vocals, lyrics, keys, and chords that may induce debilitating sorrow in some listeners. Listener discretion is advised."

I don't remember the actual song, only the abject melancholy that flooded through me upon hearing Rogers' spare guitar and soulful baritone waft over the crowd of happy, paint-faced children, batik peddlers, and poutine eaters wandering amid the waving tulips. No one else seemed particularly bothered by the dissonance between song and scene, but all I wanted to do was escape down to the riverbank and weep.

It wasn't the first, nor last, time a piece of randomly encountered music would ambush me and amplify my sadness, almost unbearably. Once, it was the mournful saw of violins accompanying a video at the Canadian Museum of Civilization about early logging. Or it could be a Rufus Wainwright song sneaking up on me from the car radio. I soon became hypervigilant at recognizing that first down spiral of mood and adept at the quick lunge for the off button. Music, once a comfort and a source of pleasure, had become a minefield.

Sensitivity to sad music was just one troublesome symptom of what was eventually diagnosed as clinical depression. It was only after many months of taking citalopram, an antidepressant known as a selective serotonin reuptake inhibitor, that I realized the sad-music thing wasn't happening to me anymore. When I was puttering in the kitchen one morning with the radio on, the sound of a violin stopped me. It was "Field of Stars," by the late Oliver Schroer, a song recorded during his seven-week walk along Europe's ancient pilgrim trail, the Camino de Santiago. His wailing fiddle, echoing through an old stone chapel, made me sit down and cry—but they were the cathartic, opening kind of tears.

Soon I stopped fearing music, maudlin TV commercials, and Animal Planet programs about cruelty to chimpanzees. I was still able to feel sadness, but I was not so overwhelmed by the emotion. And I became curious: exactly what was going on in my brain to make me so vulnerable to music in the first place—and why was a pill able to change all that?

Antidepressants, we know, affect the activity of neurotransmitters such as serotonin, dopamine, and norepinephrine, and hormones such as oxytocin, all of which are involved in the experience of pleasure. These are the hormones that become seriously impaired when a person is depressed. But what is the specific link—if any—between mood and musical expression? Searching for answers, I turned first to the neuroscience of music, a thriving field of research that has

spawned two current best sellers—Oliver Sacks' *Musicophilia: Tales of Music and the Brain*, a collection of strange tales about the human relationship to music, and Daniel Levitin's *This Is Your Brain on Music: The Science of a Human Obsession*, which details recent neurological findings. Among them: what's happening in the brain when music uplifts us; why bits of music can lodge in the brain (the dreaded "earworm" or "tune cootie"); and theories of how and why music—in all its pitches, tempos, keys, and rhythms—has played an integral role in the evolution of the human species.

Levitin is a psychology professor who runs the Laboratory for Music Perception, Cognition, and Expertise at McGill University. Before becoming a psychologist, he was a session musician, sound engineer, and record producer for the likes of Santana and Blue Öyster Cult. When I call him on the phone, he sits down at the piano in his Montreal home and plays a riff of trilling high notes, followed by a slow series of notes lower down the scale. It makes the obvious point that what we think of as sad music tends to be quieter, lower, and slower, with longer duration in tones

50 utne NOV-DEC '08

NOV-DEC '08 utne 51

ava gardner

CIGARETTE IN ONE HAND, GLASS OF SCOTCH IN THE OTHER,

Classic film siren Ava Gardner was hardly the type of actress to court respectability — on screen or off. Raised dirt-poor on a North Carolina tobacco farm, she was discovered in 1941 after her brother-in-law displayed her photo in his New York shop. Ava's first screen test was a dud, but MGM took the bait anyway with starry-eyed visions of Metro-Girl moulding. She can't act. She can't talk. She's terrific.

Frustrated at first as little more than a pretty piece of flesh with an un-couth southern accent to boot, Ava smuggled an ex-lover through the over-30 barrier — one of an endless line of drop-dead-dapper romances used to lure the chiselled-cheek set to big kids. During this time she fobbed her studio contract by posing for hundreds of cheesecake pin-up shots that focused on her body and legs rather than her figure. Ava still her femme fatale turn in *Pandora and the Flying Dutchman*.

From here on, the public's object is complimented on the face that would root her branded in the "No.xxx The World's Most Beautiful Animal," and typically self-deprecating, Ava taught herself to remodel on demand. I have enough talent scouts among the MGM crewe get a to meet the North Pole. Ava made her face and her body were too complex. Deep down, I'm pretty superficial! Thy frequently took on roles demanding smart beauty, as a Columbia stature come to life in *the Touch of Venus*, a singer with man leg, and the fort in *Pandora and the Flying Dutchman*.

By the time Ava's star was on the rise, she had already been married twice — to Mickey Rooney in 1942 and bandleader Artie Shaw in 1945. But it was her heralded union of Frank Sinatra that plunged her worldwide. In the scarlet woman for supposedly tempting the Catholic Sinatra away from his first wife Nancy, Ava was condemned by the church, vilified by the Legion of Decency and labelled "Bitch." Another "Sadness", by notorious art form. The union was passionate but volatile. We were always good in bed, Ava later admitted. This couple usually started on the way to the train. After a head-rattling jigger to drink before. Yet the Sinatra-Gardner drama and accusations of adultery, Ava and Sinatra finally split in 1957.

Thirty years earlier, Ava had travelled to Spain to film *The Barefoot Contessa*, the story of a Spanish courtesan made into a screen star and fought over by multitudes, who's terrace photographed by the trappings of fame and money. It's a tale of Tinseltello gone wrong, made comfortable all the time by combining the pair among the humanes race down and one that seemed to mirror Gardner's own. After watching the film, Ava purchased a great passion for Spain and subsequently an even greater taste for application of entertainers and bullfighters. The country became her home after her third marriage, though with bullrings at heart, along the bullfights. For the years that focus of the Spains, wherever Ava went and wherever she did, she was still pining for Sinatra, or struggling with some great love connoi.

Working on ever stronger cast, Ava became, by the look, funny, for the past. Ava later career saw her making movies only intermittently to take in a big-budget flicks like *On the Beach* or *The Night of the Iguana*, sometimes self-financed by deep devotion, in budget riffles. With no free-age chopping up Ava Hamilton, London in the late 1960s, and was done with her beach in 1990. I don't mind growing old, Ava once said. It's hard to get before the time I'll go — cigarette in one hand, glass of scotch in the other.

The standard assessment of Ava Gardner is that she was a ruin to actress who happening in the pop beauty. But Ava never played the type of roles that garner respectability for an actress, nor did she appear in films that win prizes and actual acclaim. Nominated several times for high profile awards, she continually lost out to awards. If an actress consumed more reputable, more respectable instead, Ava worked in the same moves of the movie industry — in melodramas, historical romances and jungle movies, in mute films and westerns — hardly the stuff to make for a classic, sterling gal. The public sized her too. While her beauty and the scandals of her private life distracted attention from Ava's work, they strengthened her box-office pull and made her a bankable star. And through it all, the tobacco farmer's daughter retained her earthy sense of humour. To the end, her favourite introduction was: Honey, don't you know who I am? I'm a lousy movie star. •

'I would suggest requesting a portfolio review and/or dropping off a portfolio. I would not recommend only targeting the creative director of a magazine as they are often too busy to look at junior designer books. I think that it is better to target the second in command as well.'

Jennifer Pastore, Associate Photo Editor, *T: The New York Times Style Magazine*

Scanning for innovation

Global plastics company Rehau looks to a small team of 'innovation scouts' in procurement to harvest the most promising ideas from its key suppliers

by Geraint John

Unless you work in the construction, automotive or furniture industries, the chances are you won't have heard of Rehau. As a family-owned manufacturer of plastic products such as window frames, water pipes and car bumpers, it isn't the kind of firm that excites much interest from the general business press. But as an example of how procurement can extend its role into the field of innovation and drive company competitiveness, it has an interesting story to tell – one that throws up some useful lessons for CPOs and their teams in other sectors.

Founded in 1948 in the German town of Rehau, from which it takes its name, the firm now has operations in over 40 locations around the world, employing almost 15,000 staff and earning annual revenues in excess of €2 billion. Over time, Rehau has moved away from simply making plastic products of its own to assembling water heating and other systems that incorporate parts from other manufacturers. This is vital for the company's long-term survival because some of its products, particularly in the construction industry, which accounts for half its total business, have been commoditised as a result of strong competition from China and elsewhere.

As might be expected of a German manufacturer, Rehau's strategy is not to be the lowest-cost producer, explains Rainer Schulz, the company's chief operating officer, but to show "innovation, process and service leadership". That means not only being highly efficient in purchasing, production and logistics terms, he says, but also having "cleverer products than our competitors".

With around 50 in-house researchers, Rehau is used to inventing what Schulz describes as 'new recipes' for polymers such as polyvinyl chloride (PVC), polypropylene and polyethylene – its key raw materials – and then working with chemical companies, big and small, to manufacture them. But to satisfy the needs of its customers today, it must be effective at tapping the innovative ideas of these and other key suppliers and translating them into marketable products, some of which will be developed jointly.

Nowhere is the pressure to innovate stronger than in the automotive industry, from which Rehau derives another 30 per cent of its revenues. As a first-tier supplier to the likes of Daimler, BMW, Volkswagen, Toyota and General Motors, the company not only has to meet stringent cost, quality and delivery targets, but also demonstrate that it is at the forefront of technological change.

However, notes Schulz, in the past the image of Rehau as an innovator was not one that many of its customers recognised. A customer survey four years ago found that "it was not seen as an innovative company, it was seen as a big oil tanker, driven one way and very hard to change", he says. As a result, Rehau decided to rebrand itself with a new tagline, 'unlimited polymer solutions', and to introduce an internal change programme designed to get employees in its key functions, including procurement, better focused on innovation.

Enter the innovation scout

To aid internal co-ordination and boost interaction with its supply base, in 2004 Rehau introduced a new role in its 140-strong procurement network – that of 'innovation scout'. It is one of six core roles in the function (see figure 1), which is organised around the material group (or category) management structure implemented by Schulz three years earlier when he joined the company from BMW. Rolls-Royce as head of materials management and logistics. (As COO, Schulz retains overall responsibility for purchasing, as

Opposite: The Internet allows art directors to have their pick of international talent. Conceptual illustrator, Michelle Thompson, is not just reliant on clients from her native Britain for work. Pictured here are commissions for Canada's *The Globe and Mail* newspaper (top) and customer magazine, *CPO Agenda* (bottom), published by Redactive Media.

Below: Spreads from tri-lingual in-flight magazines, *b.spirit!* (top), and *b.there!* (bottom), produced for Brussels Airlines by Ink Publishing. Aimed at long- and short-haul passengers respectively, the publications are designed with a contemporary feel and make extensive use of striking imagery.

Illustration commissions

The editorial sector tends to be the one that provides most illustrators with their first commissions. The relationship between art editors and fledgling illustrators is a symbiotic one, with hitherto unpublished artists getting much-needed exposure in exchange for relatively modest fees – editorial clients rarely have access to the kind of funds wielded by design companies and advertising agencies. Turnover is fast, which means the illustrators get into print quickly. Editorial clients, meanwhile, get their pick of emerging talent, thus keeping their publications looking fresh and cutting-edge; a win-win situation.

Crucially, the editorial commissioning process is very direct. You show your work to the art editor, who is paid to make the publication look good and has the budget to do just that. If illustrations are a regular feature and the commissioner takes a shine to your work, you're in with a pretty good chance – subject to a nod from the editor. Given that, overall, magazines and newspapers cover every subject under the sun, the more areas you choose to make your own in the editorial arena, the more scope you will have to earn serious money later on. And, between them, editorial clients use just about every illustrative style there is.

Although art editors have sometimes tended to view an in-house designer with illustrative skills with suspicion, at the time of writing there is a lot of interest in hand-lettering so, if your illustration work has a typographic component this may be a plus when it comes to obtaining commissions. However, because most magazines employ in-house designers and work to existing grids, there is little chance you will be used in a full-on design capacity. On the other hand, there are instances where both freelance and full-time designers are asked to provide illustrations for the magazines that employ them – though, in the case of full-timers, they are often expected to produce these in their own time. Trade magazines or ones with a limited readership (and, by extension, budget) are more likely than other publications to get illustrations done in-house by a cross-disciplinary practitioner.

'As I commission illustration on a regular basis I am looking for original ideas and illustration which would compliment or work alongside other more established illustrators. I receive samples from an international base of illustrators, in particular America and Europe, and occasionally Australia and Japan.'

Alison Lawn, Art Editor, *New Scientist*

Below: The first nine issues of *Varoom* magazine, published by the Association of Illustrators, were designed by Norwegian/British partnership Non-Format to appeal to a visually-literate readership of practitioners, commissioners and educators. Published three times a year this issue, featuring an illustration by Brad Holland, is from 2008.

Below: *The Illustrated Ape* is an eclectic and idiosyncratic publication devoted to original fiction, poetry, pictures and pop. Each issue is themed and guest art-directed. Contributors are not paid, as proceeds go towards funding the next edition; consequently they are given a lot of creative freedom.

The Illustrated Ape ®

The Heavenly Issue

**Nicky Wire & Manic Street Preachers
The Chemical Brothers/Paul Cannell
St Etienne/Jeff Barrett/Pete Fowler
Phill Jupitus/Al Murphy/Stella Vine
Rob Ryan/Marcus Oakley/Salena Godden
Anthony Burrill/Vivian Stanshall**

ISSN 1368-2954
9 771368 295049

PRICE: £5.00
ISSUE #25

Below: Illustrators specializing in quirky
hand-rendered text are currently in vogue
with publishers, both for literary and some
mass-market fiction. Shown here are
(top) three covers by Harriet Russell for
Hodder Headline, Orion Publishing and
HarperCollins; and (bottom) two covers by
Andy Robert Davies for Summersdale
Publishers, and Nigel Owen's cover for
Faber & Faber.

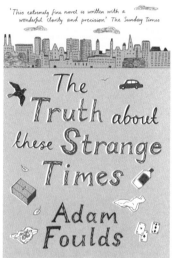

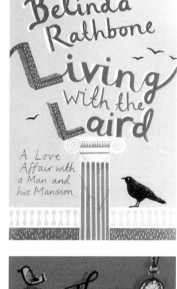

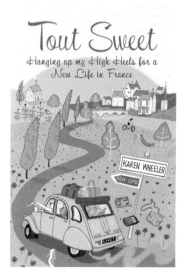

Book Publishing

Book publishing is a broad church that encompasses hardback and paperback fiction and non-fiction for all age groups. The majority of publishers routinely produce books in print and digital form for download onto PC, tablet, mobile phone or eReader. Though increasingly, as the latter become more sophisticated, more are becoming involved in the development of interactive projects, though not necessarily their production. It provides work for a diverse range of practitioners, including those with multiple skills. In the United Kingdom, some freelance book designers choose to utilize their image-making skills where appropriate, while illustrators with a strong affinity for type are currently popular with book-jacket commissioners.

'At (entry) level we expect a certain amount of educating to be needed. Budgets and deadlines being what they are, the designer needs to be up to speed as soon as possible, but there is time to develop their understanding of the industry and the language of design.'

Richard Ogle, Art Director, Random House

Starting as a book designer

Book publishers are generally happy to employ recent design graduates and some degree of nurturing is usually possible – downsized art departments notwithstanding – as the pace of book publishing is usually slightly less frenetic than that of the editorial sector. As with magazine and newspaper publishing, however, an internship or published work related to books will stand you in good stead.

Junior design positions are advertised in the creative press, on websites that specialize in creative recruitment (and, in many cases, on the publisher's own website), and in local and national newspapers (generally on days specifically devoted to creative and media jobs). Some publishers will see designers who approach them speculatively, though they may only do so if there is an actual vacancy.

A genuine interest in books – and reading – is obviously a prerequisite and, as with magazine design, you will need to think carefully about the areas to which your interests and design skills are best suited. If, for instance, you would prefer to work with photographers rather than illustrators, children's picture books are probably not the milieu for you; and if you'd rather spend quality time with Andy McNab than Thomas Pynchon, it would be sensible to steer clear of literary book covers. However, if you're planning to make your mark as a mass-market book-cover designer, remember that you're unlikely to work in just one genre and that a historical bodice-ripper can't be packaged in the same way as a psychological thriller. It is not unheard of for book designers to change their area of specialization: one of my first agency clients began by designing book jackets for adult fiction and now enjoys an immensely successful career as an art director in children's books. It pays to be adaptable, especially if you're planning to ultimately go freelance.

Many freelance book designers start off working for mainstream publishing houses, where they learn about the industry and make contacts as they progress to more senior design positions. Large publishing houses often commission freelancers and if you have networked successfully you won't have to start wooing their art directors from scratch. It's not always plain sailing, though; the chances of having a design rejected are higher than they would be if you were working in-house, as the commissioner may ask several freelancers to pitch for the same project. However, if you are a cross-disciplinary practitioner and/or have developed a recognizable style, being your own boss will provide more opportunities for you to use your skills than working as an in-house designer. Plus, you have the option of promoting these skills in creative sectors other than book publishing.

'I have occasionally produced an illustration, done a bit of photography (very basic) and created some hand-lettering when necessary, usually when the budget dictates. I think it is very helpful and attractive to be able to offer to the client all aspects of what is required to produce a finished cover.'

Lucy Bennett, freelance book-cover designer

Opposite: A true cross-disciplinary practitioner, picture-book illustrator Adolie Day also designs children's textiles, greetings cards and giftware, and sells prints of her work online. Featured are (from top, left to right) *La Merelle* stationery; the cover of her 2008 children's book, *Le Chasseur de Papillons* (The Butterfly Hunter, published by Toucan Editions); a spread from the same title; and one from her popular series of Lilichou books (published by Amaterra/ Nouvel Angle).

Children's books

The children's book market covers everything from early learning for babies and toddlers to lavish, full-colour picture books, and novels and anthologies for older readers that usually feature black-and-white line illustrations throughout.

One trend that is emerging worldwide is for more heavily illustrated texts specifically aimed at boys in the eight-plus age group, in the hope of encouraging them to read as voraciously as their female counterparts. Illustrations also frequently feature on book jackets for young adults.

Designing a picture book (or, for that matter, the interior of any book involving the juxtaposition of type and image) involves the ability to think sequentially and an understanding of visual pace in order to engage and maintain a child's attention. It also requires an innate understanding of the illustrative styles and types of layout most likely to appeal to younger age groups. Versatility, strong typographical skills, flair and imagination are all prerequisites, along with a thorough working knowledge of QuarkXPress, InDesign, Photoshop and, possibly, Illustrator.

No matter what trends prevail elsewhere in publishing, children's books can be relied upon to provide work for illustrators whose style is suitable for a younger demographic. Whatever the age group that is being targeted, an illustrator's portfolio needs to show that they have sound underlying drawing skills and are capable of developing and sustaining strong, appealing and, above all, distinctive characters that children in the relevant age group will relate to. This is a lot easier said than done; I have seen many a picture-book proposal where the young protagonist ages or drops a few years virtually every time a page is turned or where the alien/monster continually – and unintentionally – changes size or shape. You will need a keen appreciation of what is happening elsewhere in the market and, at risk of stating the obvious, it helps in the long term if you can draw children and babies – though there are illustrators who have built their careers on an ability to portray animals engagingly. It is worth noting that some markets differ from others. European picture books tend to be geared towards a much younger age group (the under-sevens), than those produced by United States publishers (the under-twelves), which allow for more sophisticated imagery.

Publishers' lives are made infinitely easier by author– illustrators who provide both the text and the art for picture books. Because author–illustrators are responsible for both words and images, they tend to have a strong idea of how their books should look – which also makes the designer's job a little easier. Although there is always work for illustrators who aren't interested in writing, good picture-book illustrators far outnumber good authors, and publishers are always on the lookout for fresh stories with universal appeal. If you have a fabulous idea for a story but feel your writing is too weak to make it fly, a canny publisher can provide the encouragement and guidance to help you realize your idea.

Educational publishing

The design skills needed to work in this sector are similar to those needed in picture-book designers, though not all educational books are aimed at children. For those that are, clear, easy legibility is paramount, as is an understanding of visual imagery likely to appeal to younger age groups. Flash skills, in addition to the usual software, are also required as many educational publishers specialize in interactive work.

Aspiring children's book illustrators often get their first breaks in educational publishing, where competition is less steep. Subject matter is extremely varied and includes fiction and poetry in addition to non-fiction. However, educational books rarely pay as well as children's book publishers, or offer the same kind of recognition; they also tend to have shorter deadlines and tighter, more prescriptive briefs. With illustrators skilled enough to make the grade elsewhere routinely taking off for greener pastures, educational publishers tend to be a little less fussy than their mainstream counterparts; for instance, depending on the project, they place less emphasis on distinctiveness of character than publishers who solely commission picture books.

Although this market can serve as a springboard for illustrators hoping to make their mark in picture books, it is by no means geared only towards children. Many educational books, including dictionaries, reference and textbooks are aimed at adults, such as professionals or students in further and higher education, or people with learning disabilities. They can therefore accommodate a considerably wider variety of full-colour and black-and-white styles than children's books.

'I hire unpublished illustrators once in a while, but they need a great portfolio… The advantages are that you get something really fresh, that's not on anything else out there, and you can also mould them a bit. They tend to be really enthusiastic as well. The problem is that they often don't have their real-world skills yet, so you have to be fairly patient.'

Steve Scott, Art Director, Scholastic

Below: Publishers are always on the
lookout for strong black-and-white linework
to appeal to the 8–11-year-old age group.
This David Roberts illustration is for *The
Lepidoctor*, one of Mick Jackson's 'Ten Sorry
Tales' published by Faber & Faber in 2005.

Below: Work by the Portuguese illustrator André da Loba reveals his bright, playful 3-D style which makes him ideal for picture-book work. Featured are (from top) the cover; finished spreads; and dummy rough spreads for the picture book *El Oso y el Cuervo* (The Bear and the Crow), published by OQO Editoria.

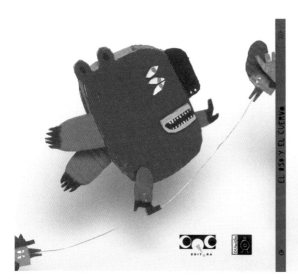

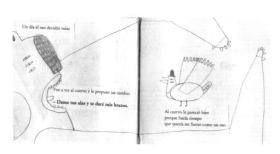

Below: Examples of illustrations for fiction
and non-fiction title covers include (top row)
design by Liam Relph with illustration by
Christopher Wormell (published by Square
Peg); two designs in the same series by
David Wardle (published by Hodder &
Stoughton); (bottom row) illustration/design
by Liam Relph (published by Harvill Secker);
design by Henry Steadman (Headline
Publishing), and cover by Meg Paradise of
Mucca Design (Rizzoli).

Opposite: Unlike many in-house
designers, cross-disciplinary freelancer
Henry Steadman often enjoys the creative
freedom to produce unusual, striking
cover designs (for Orion Publishing).

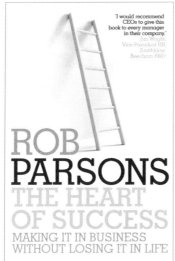

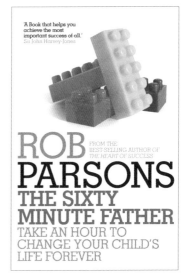

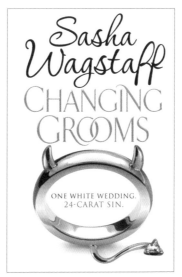

'An illustrator who can combine great image-making with well-crafted typography and hand-lettering can be useful.'

Eleanor Crow, Art Director, The Folio Society

Adult fiction

Software skills needed for book-cover design are primarily QuarkXPress (though some publishers are starting to move away from this nowadays), InDesign, Photoshop and Illustrator. Compared to designing an entire type and image-heavy book, book-jacket design is relatively straightforward, being somewhat more of a condensed process – though turnover is also appreciably faster. Versatility, strong typographical skills, the ability to use different kinds of visual imagery and a keen awareness of how different genres are packaged are all integral to the role of jacket designer. Many book-cover designers work in-house though once they have built up a good portfolio and some industry contacts, some do opt to go freelance, particularly if they are multi-skilled or have a preference for packaging certain types of literature.

Regrettably, apart from vanity publishing, the educational market or exclusive book clubs such as the United Kingdom's Folio Society, adult fiction provides little scope for illustrators. Artists with an interest in adult-themed narrative work are largely restricted to creating images for book covers. Mass-market genres, such as historical romances, sci-fi, fantasy, horror, chick lit or thrillers, are more likely to sell than literary fiction, so most publishers therefore produce rather less of this and do so in significantly smaller numbers. A mass-market novel by a popular author, for example, might enjoy a print run of 400,000 copies, whereas the one for a first novel by a young unknown might be only 4,000. Correspondingly, mass-market book covers tend to pay better than literary ones, though they tend to feature less imaginative illustrations.

Mass-market covers can be formulaic, and often look similar for years on end (the publisher is aiming to shift hundreds of thousands of books and if a tried and tested formula works…), whereas the packaging of literary fiction is more likely to reflect prevailing design and illustration trends. If your work is more stylized than highly realistic, and narrative is your thing, this is the area for you, but the comparatively small output means there is a lot of competition. Since freelance designers tend to have smaller budgets than those employed by publishers, many take advantage of photo libraries and royalty-free stock to keep production costs to a minimum. Illustrators are best advised to contact literary-fiction designers working in-house.

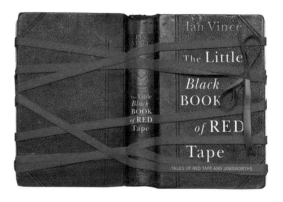

Adult non-fiction

Despite the target audience, the skills needed to work in this sector are very similar to those needed for picture-book design (see page 48). Depending on the type of publication, the length of time spent in production might vary. A book that ties in with a television series, for instance, may have a tighter schedule.

Although adult non-fiction, particularly when it is lifestyle related, is frequently heavily illustrated, photography is often the preferred medium. This can be because of prevailing trends, subject matter, or simply the publisher. For example, publishers who specialize in cheap and cheerful editions can minimize production costs by reusing photographs to which they already own the rights, whereas more upmarket ones are likely to commission new work. A book written by a celebrity chef, interior designer or fitness guru is more likely to feature photographs than illustrations, especially if the author is photogenic. Nonetheless, given the wide-ranging subject matter – from football to car maintenance to transcendental meditation – there are opportunities for illustrators, particularly for those with highly specialized illustration skills, such as botanical, medical and natural history artists, and those who specialize in maps, diagrams, room or garden plans and 'step-by-step' illustrations.

Below: Even in an era where a myriad of
fonts are downloadable at the click of a
mouse, there is still a demand for classic
calligraphy in publishing. Here, lettering
is by illustrator/calligrapher Peter Horridge
and design by Eleanor Ridsdale (for
Laurence King Publishing).

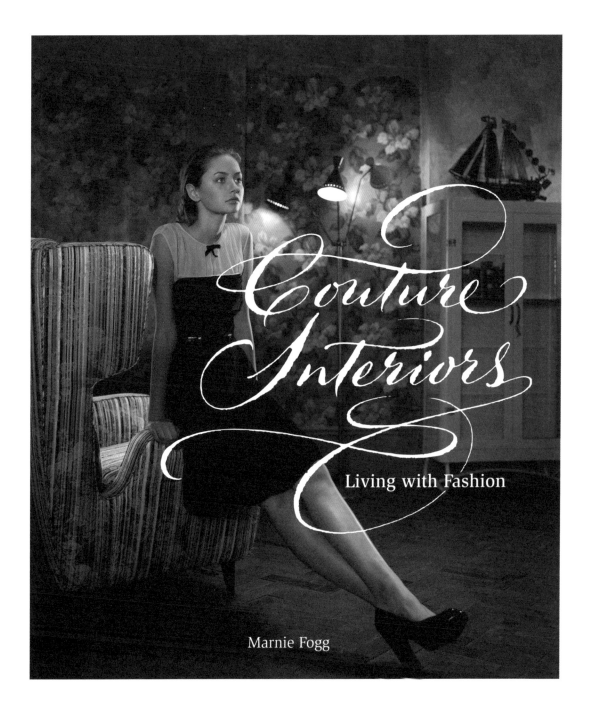

Couture Interiors

Living with Fashion

Marnie Fogg

Below: The cover for this contemporary edition of the *Bible* (top) was illustrated by Steve Wilson (for Hodder & Stoughton), proof that a fresh visual approach can breathe life into the oldest of subject matter; (bottom) Rafael Nobre is a Brazilian-based freelancer who combined his design and illustration skills to striking effect for this book-cover commission (for Editora Record).

'Comics are a narrative art form... It is not enough to draw: a sense of space and time, of dynamics, page layout and typography as well as the unique visual vocabulary of comics must also be understood (thought balloons, motion lines, etc.) and employed. This is why editors want to see pages of comics and not merely illustrations of characters.'

Steven Preston, comic author, artist and publisher

Opposite: Many independent comic-book artists have parallel careers as commercial illustrators. Chloe Noonan's creator, Marc Ellerby, services a number of music industry clients. A firm supporter of the small press, Marc has worked on several solo projects in addition to work for Oni Press and Image Comics.

Overleaf: Nobrow is an independent, European publisher dedicated to keeping the art of print alive. Specializing in high quality comics, books and graphic novels, they work on an invitation-only basis with a wide variety of contemporary graphic artists and illustrators – from talented newcomers to well-established veterans.

Comics and Graphic Novels

There are two paths into the comics and graphic novels world, and whether you take the independent or the commercial route, the kind of living you are able to make will largely depend on where you are based and/or where you promote your work. Some countries, most notably France, Japan and the United States, have larger markets than others, and these can differ according to the prevailing culture. Meanwhile, in Japan and in European countries, with the exception of the United Kingdom, even mainstream comics aren't considered the exclusive province of young children and adolescent boys; genres are varied and publications are geared towards both genders and a wide variety of age groups. Apart from the independent comics scene, this is not generally the case in America or Britain. Indeed, despite wholeheartedly embracing the manga style, in the United Kingdom comics are viewed primarily as a medium for the subteen market.

Depending on the type of work you produce, and your dedication to the genre, you may have to look to foreign markets, or even additional ones – such as storyboarding for film and television, character development for computer games and animation, or the less specialized areas of editorial and publishing – to supplement your income.

Independent comics, being largely self-authored and self-published, do not provide opportunities for graphic designers. If they do become successful enough for a commercial publisher to show interest, an in-house designer or freelancer will be responsible for the design. Commercial comic publishers, however, employ graphic designers in the same capacity that regular editorial publishers do. Designers or illustrators with an interest in designing letterforms are also commissioned by comic-book publishers.

The independent route

Independent comics are mostly self-authored with complete artistic control maintained by the creator, who also owns the rights to the work subject to any terms subsequently offered by a publisher, assuming he or she is fortunate enough to find one. Publishers – even if they are specialists with an interest in quirky graphic novels – are in it for the money, and won't consider publishing anything that doesn't already have a significant readership. It is, therefore, up to the self-publisher to reach as wide an audience as possible before approaching a commercial publisher.

This can be done in a variety of ways: through dedicated comic shops, independent and art bookshops, or even funky clothes shops and music stores – businesses like these usually agree to take publications on a sale or return basis. Independent distribution networks can supply shops outside your geographical area and/or will market your work online – though there is nothing to stop you selling, or even publishing, it online yourself, and many do. Some distributors function as limited-edition publishers, and produce very small home-made print runs, while small-press book fairs and indie comic conventions, such as the long-running, well-attended annual event held in Angoulême in southern France, or the Small Press Expo in Maryland in the United States, attract collectors and provide opportunities to network with fellow creators, distributors and writers looking for artists to collaborate with.

Illustrators who succeed in finding a commercial publisher are often rewarded by seeing their earlier, self-published efforts produced as anthologies, thereby reaching a very much larger readership. Though some go on to penetrate the mainstream, with film adaptations and related collectable merchandise, the independent comics arena is not generally lucrative, and even the most successful creators have to work outside it if they are hoping to make a full-time living as artists.

The commercial route

Commercial comics are another story. The illustrator (hired on a freelance basis and usually working from home) generally has little personal creative input and works as part of a team, collaborating with writers, lettering artists, etc., on stories about characters to which the publisher and/or originator owns the rights. Many are tie-ins to sci-fi, fantasy or action films and television shows; the superhero genre is particularly popular in France and the United States. Styles are widely varied, with publishers constantly on the lookout for new ways to breathe life into old favourites. Industry behemoths Marvel and DC loom large worldwide and have the pick of the very best artists, so competition is stiff – not least in the United Kingdom where there are significantly fewer publishers of comics and graphic novels than elsewhere. Whatever your style, your figure and character work must be strong and consistent; likewise your sequential drawing skills. It is particularly important that you are able to draw the characters that feature in the comics you are hoping to work for.

Large commercial comic conventions, such as those held in Bristol and Birmingham in England offer anyone who is keen to break into the market a chance to meet publishers informally and attend talks by leading comic artists who are working in

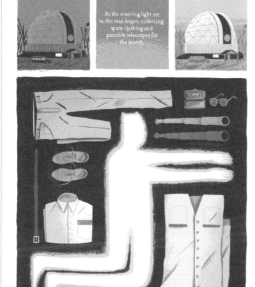

'Considering the amount of raw comics talent in Britain, there are still relatively few outlets, and gaining success can be a long daunting slog. Hop across the channel to France or Spain though, and you'll find countries who wholeheartedly embrace the world of comics and the markets are seriously thriving.'

Boo Cook, comic artist

a wide variety of genres. Some conventions also offer the facility for artists to get feedback on their portfolios from guest professionals, and I have known several illustrators who have picked up comparatively well-paid commissions by going to these events. Although the conventions tend to attract a different kind of clientele to the indie and small-press ones, there is nothing to stop self-publishers hiring a stand to introduce their work to a wider readership – but be prepared to make a loss.

In addition to industry trade fairs there are online resources that give details of publishers in different parts of the world. Be aware, however, that submission guidelines vary; some may solicit only finished projects while others may simply want to see relevant samples of your style. It is always advisable to contact the companies to determine their requirements.

Because it's hard to make a reliable living as an illustrator of comics or graphic novels, even in the commercial sector, remember that other types of publication favour a sequential approach to storytelling. Many educational publishers use comic-book styles to appeal to adolescents with significantly lower reading ages, or to make books that might otherwise be considered a bit dull more interesting to older children, particularly boys. Manga-style Shakespeare or classic literature retold as graphic novels are becoming increasingly commonplace. There is even a manga-style Bible. Magazines, including junior titles, frequently run comic strips, so if you have the will and inspiration this could also be a way of raising your profile.

Opposite: Some of commercial comic-book artist Boo Cook's work for monthly comic, *Elephantmen* (top) and its mini-series *War Toys* (bottom). Successful comics are often later anthologized in trade paperback form, which can result in additional related commissions.

Below: Until the publication of her novel, *The Time Traveler's Wife*, Audrey Niffenegger was primarily known as a painter and printmaker. *The Three Incestuous Sisters* (for The Random House Group Ltd), was originally self-published in a limited edition of 10 handmade books, and took 14 years to complete.

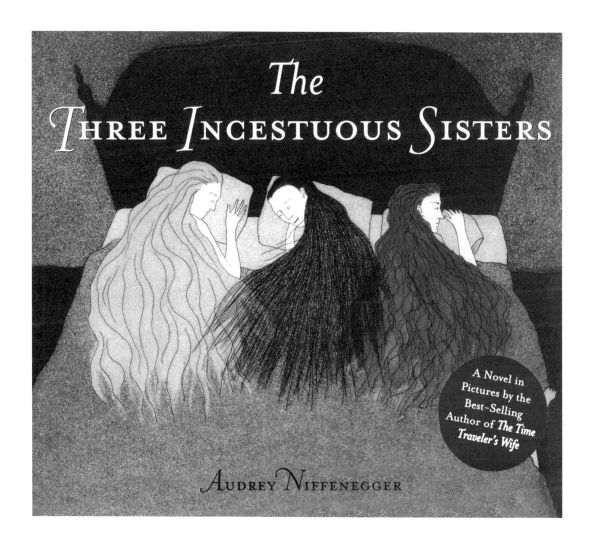

Television and Film

As mentioned earlier in this chapter, certain design groups and branding consultancies specialize in serving the needs of the entertainment industry. Needless to say, because this is something of a niche market, there is competition to work in television and film.

'Size of company is an important factor but I also believe a young designer can find a healthy, nurturing experience in a wide range of work settings.'
Doug Powell, Creative Director, Schwartz Powell Design

Opportunities for designers

Branding work undertaken on behalf of a television network could involve the creation of a channel identity or the rebranding of a tired one. Trailers, title sequences, idents and brand campaigns that promote specific programmes or channels can all fall within the broadcast designer's remit, and it's not unheard of for some designers to take on directorial roles. In contrast, television companies employ relatively few graphic designers and, since the majority of programmes are bought in complete with title sequences from the production companies that made them, in-house designers are likely to be employed to produce graphics for local productions, such as the news (the BBC has a dedicated news-graphics department), or trailers.

Designers with a particular interest in motion graphics are best off targeting broadcast-design specialists or production companies. However, the latter could offer less in the way of creative freedom and satisfaction, as the graphic designer's role is primarily technical and mostly involves putting directors' ideas into practice rather than implementing their own. Consequently, at entry level, production houses place much more emphasis on software skills than do design companies, who are principally concerned with ideas and creative problem solving.

Design for the film industry can also involve motion graphics, generally in making trailers or editing existing ones. There is also plenty of affiliated print and web-based work, such as posters, flyers, and press and web advertisements promoting theatrical and home entertainment releases; websites dedicated to the promotion of individual films; and, lastly, design for DVD packaging and point-of-sale.

My advice for accessing job opportunities in both television and film is: research (there are various publications and online directories that list production companies and provide links to their websites); internships; competitions; networking; watching out for advertisements; and keeping up to date with developments in your chosen sector. It goes without saying that your portfolio – or show reel – should adequately reflect your areas of interest and the relevant disciplines in which you are able to work.

'Generally we look for a specific range of skills and then encourage experimentation and growth in different software and techniques. Being small, and by choice, we are always multitasking. It makes for a more interesting process. Everyone in our team turns their hands at different methods and techniques while specializing in a core set of skills.'
Judy Wellfare, Creative Director, Plus et Plus

Below: Bahn TV is the customer-orientated German TV channel of the German National Railway company Deutsche Bahn AG (now solely available online). Idents, like this one created by Berlin-based broadcast designer Sascha Verwiebe, are part of the broadcast designer's remit – along with trailers, title sequences and brand campaigns.

Below: Since its inclusion on Ladyhawke's debut album, Australian artist Sarah Larnach's artwork have become synonymous with the musician's visual identity. The stills are from the promo for single *My Delirium* in which the artist's signature style was animated. The film was directed by partnership Frater, from Partizan Lab for Modular Recordings.

Opportunities for illustrators

Illustration is rarely commissioned for broadcast channel identities – since logos and idents can be used for some years, the network concerned would either have to purchase the copyright to the artwork, or keep renewing its licence to use it, which some find irksome. Illustration in film promotion is largely a matter of fashion; at the time of writing very little is used outside promoting small, independent art-house releases or the occasional retro pastiche. Most illustration work tends to be specialized and production companies regularly employ freelance storyboard and concept artists. Like design groups, these companies can vary tremendously when it comes to the sectors they target and their individual areas of expertise. Thus, in addition to film and television programmes, a storyboard artist working for a diverse range of production companies could potentially be involved in the development of commercials; music promos; corporate, educational or training videos; or audio-visuals for live events.

Storyboards

Essentially there are two kinds of storyboard. The first sets the visual tone for a film, promo, title sequence or advertisement. In the case of films, it's the production company's job to raise financial backing for a project prior to coordinating it, and these highly finished, full-colour, pre-production visuals play a vital part in this process. (It's not unusual for a budding film-maker to approach a storyboard artist before they approach a production company.) A montage of images relating to key sequences also enables a director to talk a client through a project during the early stages of its conception. Depending on sector and geographical location, this pre-production storyboard is alternatively known as a client board or a mood board and is, as its name suggests, more concerned with ambience than technical details.

The second type – sometimes called a shooting board – fulfils an altogether different purpose. Entirely concerned with technical and directorial details, it provides a frame-by-frame breakdown of the action, right down to close-ups and camera angles, and is strictly adhered to by the crew during production. Consequently, it's generally rendered in black and white in a basic, pared-down style that can easily be photocopied. Since projects are rarely shot in sequence, the storyboard shows at a glance which scenes can be shot together in order to keep production costs down.

Some sectors suit certain personality types – and abilities – better than others. Producing a storyboard for an advertising agency may pay top dollar but you'll be expected to turn it around within a couple of days and will be allowed very little in the way of personal creative input. Conversely, producing one for a feature film can take three or four months and won't pay nearly as well; however, it's less stressful and there is an element of creativity.

Different types of client will want to see different kinds of subject matter in your portfolio. An advertising agency, for instance, will need to be convinced you can handle the mundane and everyday ('busy mum opens packet of breakfast cereal'), whereas a production company that specializes in big-budget CGI wizardry will think more along the lines of 'superhero torches vampire hordes using only the power of his mind'. As well as sound sequential drawing skills and the ability to swiftly commit the creative ideas of others to paper, you need to be able to think cinematically – so it helps to have a working knowledge of what a camera can do.

Concept art

Film production companies sometimes headhunt established illustrators who've made their name in fantasy or sci-fi with a view to their working as concept artists. Any major fantasy production employs at least one of these, and they are responsible for the overall look of a film. As with mood-setting storyboarding, this is primarily a pre-production visualization job. The concept artist works with the director and with the production designer, who heads up the art department – the people who build the sets, and design the vehicles, creatures, costumes, etc., with whom the artist liaises regularly to ensure the visuals are in synch with their vision. Anyone who is specifically seeking visualization work in film should research which productions are currently looking for crew, and contact the designer via the relevant production company. An excellent place to start is www.mandy.com, which carries advertisements for productions that are recruiting worldwide. Established illustrators who wish to be involved in general storyboarding can advertise their services for free on a number of dedicated websites.

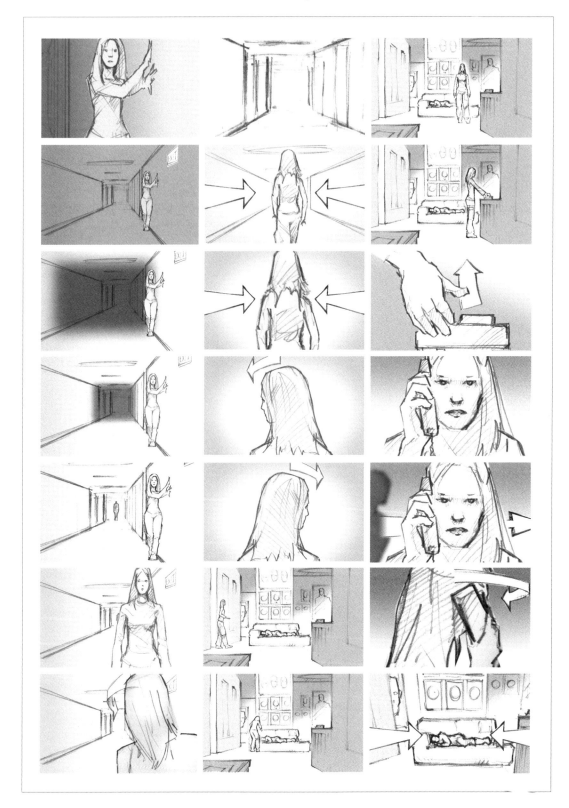

Opposite: A shooting board is concerned with technical and directorial details and typically produced in a pared-down black-and-white style. This one, created by designer, illustrator and storyboard artist, Graham Humphreys, is for the Eitan Arrusi film *Reverb* released in 2007.

Below: A detailed, atmospheric concept piece for low-budget 2008 horror film, *Flick*. Director David Howard first contacted illustrator Alex Tomlinson after seeing some of his editorial work. The job included a final poster design (bottom left), plus a period-style comic spread used in the filming of the title sequence (bottom right).

Computer Games Development

This popular, ever-expanding sector operates slightly differently from most of the others outlined in this book. Firstly, it's one of the few areas that can provide illustrators with permanent in-house or short-contract work as well as with freelance commissions. (From the developer's point of view, employing in-house artists means it is possible to exert some measure of control over highly confidential projects.) Secondly, with the industry in a growth phase and many developers operating across the globe, there are opportunities to travel.

Although graphic designers are used to package and promote games at the post-production/publishing stage, there are many more openings for artists and animators. However, depending on the company set-up and the project in hand, it can be helpful to have an illustrator or animator with additional design experience, and some developers recruit staff with combined skills – for example, an artist with experience in print or web design, as interface design, relating to the splash screens and menus, etc., takes place at the pre-production stage. Company size and ethos vary tremendously and there are no set roles; the kind of work offered and the number of artists involved is contingent on the project being developed. With roles so often overlapping, teamworking skills are essential and, as with other areas of creative employment, the ability to communicate ideas verbally as well as visually is vital to developing a strong end-product.

Illustration skills

Broadly speaking, two types of illustrator operate within games development: concept artists, who work in 2-D at the early pre-production stage; and 3-D modellers and highly specialized texture artists, who bring their concepts to life digitally. Although some artists choose to concentrate on just one area, such as characters, vehicles or environments, at entry level a variety of styles and a degree of flexibility towards subject matter is advisable. As with the majority of commissioning sectors, having a recognizable, individual style can be a strength. However, given that the look of a game may be realistic, stylized or cartoonish, the downside of having only one style is that it may not be the one a developer wants. Similarly, if you start off with a view to concentrating on one particular subject area it could take longer to gain a foothold in the industry. Look on specialization as a long- rather than short-term goal.

Despite the popularity of programs such as Paint Shop Pro and Painter, Adobe currently dominates this sector and Photoshop skills are as compulsory as excellent drawing.

Developers aren't necessarily prescriptive about how concepts are created, but if your artwork is to be involved in other aspects of development it eventually has to be compatible with whatever system is in place. If possible, get used to working with screen resolutions and the particular file formats used in digital modelling, as well as working at higher resolutions for print. In relation to games and animation, digital modelling is not to be confused with the high poly modelling used in film and television. Alias Maya, LightWave or 3ds Max are the preferred norm.

With many developers forming specific links with art establishments that offer courses in games design, curricula are being developed with an eye to providing a highly skilled workforce; therefore, graduates are in demand. Job opportunities can frequently be accessed via developers' own websites as well as through magazines and websites focused on the games industry (many of which also provide excellent careers advice), specialist recruitment agencies and online communities. There are resources for concept artists to promote their work online, sometimes for free, but some hosting sites request a year's professional experience before you do so. Once again, job placements and freelance work count towards establishing you as a professional.

Below: This Invention Suspension game was produced by Aardman Digital to promote the 'Wallace and Gromit present A World of Cracking Ideas' exhibition at the Science Museum, London. The game functioned as a viral marketing piece designed to drive traffic to the Cracking Ideas website, as well as entertain the gamers.

'The best advice to a fledgling illustrator is to be as broad as you can. A lot of people just want to be character designers but this can be quite limiting. Companies do ask for people who can illustrate environments, objects and such; as illustrators progress and prove their skill they may develop a reputation for excelling in a certain area.'

Jim Thompson, course co-ordinator, BA & MA Games Design, University of Central Lancashire, UK

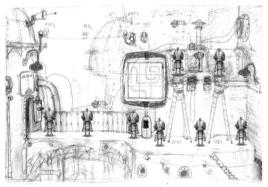

Opposite: Still from and developmental work for environment and characters featured in web game, Machinarium, in which the protagonist is a small robot. Amanita Design, independent games developer, was founded by Czech game designer and visual artist Jakub Dvorsky who has a quirky, distinctive aesthetic.

Below: Examples of character development using 3-D modelling from a student project. Initial sketches (bottom right) are used to define features, which are then transcribed for the computer using Zbrush software (top).

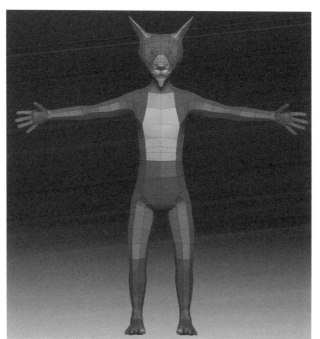

Opposite: Card designs by Andrew Pavitt (top), who originally began publishing and distributing his own cards. Discovering, however, that he preferred designing to administrative aspects of the business, his work is published by Art Angels; Rachel Harper (bottom) is one of a stable of designers working for licensing company Inspire By Design, which functions on a speculative basis, much like a textile studio.

Greetings Cards

Publishers of greetings cards vary from large-scale international operations to tiny one-man bands, and fall into two categories: those who produce cards for wholesalers and those who specialize in DTR (direct to retail). While standards in the wholesale area have risen significantly over the past few years, the cards are generally bland and multi-purpose. It is therefore preferable to target the DTR sector as the pay is better, and the work is less generic.

In-house design positions

Greetings cards form a substantial yet discrete part of the gift industry and can provide full-time employment for junior and experienced graphic designers. Jobs can be found in industry-related publications and on recruitment and job-search websites in addition to publishers' own websites, while some companies offer student internships, which are generally unpaid. Depending on the size of the company, roles can vary and some publishers state a preference for applicants with multiple or illustrative skills. Not all publishers work with illustrators; some concentrate more on photography or fine art, and a design job with one of these could involve picture research. Publishers with a reputation for illustrated cards might generate all or some of the work in-house, while others might expect a designer to commission freelance illustrators. Regardless of the kind of publisher, a strong interest in trends within the greetings card sector and a familiarity with Illustrator, Photoshop, QuarkXPress and InDesign are givens. Excellent typographic and layout skills are also key. Some card companies employ specialists in cardboard engineering, so some skills or an interest in this could stand you in good stead if you're likely to be working on pop-up/novelty cards.

Illustrating greetings cards

The greetings cards sector is one of the few commissioning areas where having multiple illustrative styles is regarded as a plus. However, the gift industry is largely speculative and illustrators of greetings cards are rarely paid for developmental work. Furthermore, unless an artist has a proven track record with a particular publisher, there is no guarantee that a projected series of cards will go ahead. If an illustrator is new to the publisher, or is working on a range that deviates significantly from the company's previous output, the publisher needs to be confident that the cards will sell before spending money on putting it into production.

The gift industry works several seasons ahead – Valentine and Easter ranges are launched in the summer of the previous year – and some card publishers give their contemporary, decorative illustrators fashion forecasts to work from. However, the visual identities of individual companies can vary tremendously, and decorative work is not the only type favoured by publishers. Other popular illustrated genres include cute/whimsical, quirky/humorous, traditional, fine art, juvenile, and handmade or hand-finished cards.

Finding the right publisher

Publishers promote their greetings cards in a variety of ways, including exhibiting them at annual national or regional trade fairs, which are held throughout the year. The fairs are attended by buyers ranging from the owners of small, independent gift shops and galleries to those representing department stores and large chains, and agents, wholesalers and overseas distributors. Any practitioner considering a career in greetings cards should find out about the industry by going to as many trade fairs as possible. This applies whether you are a designer in search of a full-time job, an illustrator looking for commissions, or want to set up a publishing enterprise of your own. Trade fairs provide the opportunity to check out hundreds of companies under one roof and see many more examples of the ranges they offer than you would by visiting individual shops. Be aware, however, that most publishers are there to sell rather than buy, and few will have the time or inclination to peruse portfolios. It's preferable to ask whether you can send them samples of your work when the fair is over.

So far as illustrators are concerned, the ideal is to work for a card publisher that employs a designer to commission artwork, as someone with a trained eye is likely to make sensible design decisions. Quality control is a good indicator of a company's ethos. Before approaching any publisher you should ensure two criteria are met: firstly, their merchandise is of a consistently high standard; and secondly, you can see your work fitting in with their aesthetic. Being on the same wavelength as your publisher means your work is less likely to be rejected, by them or the retailers that do business with them. Lastly, never be tempted to answer advertisements in non-industry publications placed by 'exciting new card companies looking for exciting new illustrators'. They are invariably cowboys or clueless start-ups – and any involvement with them is sure to end in tears.

Below: Siobhan Harrison trained
and worked in textiles before retraining
in illustration, after which she worked
in-house in the greetings card industry.
She now works in the area of children's
books and editorial illustration as well as
cards. Her adaptability has made her
popular with a wide clientele as she is able
to work across a variety of greetings card
genres, including cute and character-based
(left) and decorative (right).

Creating a portfolio

When developing a portfolio of samples to show prospective
publishers it's worth bearing in mind that, whereas many
people prefer attractive 'inside left blank for own message'
cards that reflect their taste, personality or sense of humour,
others prefer one that states the obvious, sometimes at length
or in rhyme. I have worked in retail, and was once informed
by a customer in search of a card proclaiming 'Happy Birthday
to My Wife' that this (as opposed to writing his own personal
message to said wife in a non-spouse-specific birthday card)
was 'the protocol'. I later noticed that illustrators whose
publishers had given them carte blanche to produce ranges
of blank cards had done so only after spending years in the
message-card sector, proving that they were commercial.

I therefore recommend developing a selection of small
'taster' ranges that show how you might approach common
themes: one range covering weddings, engagements and
Valentines perhaps; another, birthday cards for different ages
or family members; and another addressing pregnancy, new
babies and christenings, and so on. This will also give you
an opportunity to show off your stylistic versatility.

appeal or putting so much money into production that the
eventual retail price was prohibitively expensive.

Lastly, when it comes to selling your cards start by exhibiting
them at one of the smaller, regional gift fairs. These are more
affordable and less corporate than the major international events.

Setting up as a publisher

Whether you are a designer or an illustrator, if you are
considering becoming a card publisher yourself you will need
to give serious thought to how good your business skills are
and how you might finance the enterprise. You will spend
comparatively little time designing or illustrating; instead, you'll
be involved with the production and marketing of your range:
sourcing materials; dealing with printers; processing, packaging
up and sending out orders; engendering new business by
whatever means possible; sending out invoices and statements;
and chasing up outstanding payments – all the while juggling
your cash flow. The learning curve can be steep, and research
is of the utmost importance.

Go to gift fairs, and talk to agents, retailers and other card
publishers about your commercial viability before you even
think about putting your ideas into print. Better still, first learn
the ropes by designing or illustrating for other publishers. I
have seen inexperienced publishers make wretched business
decisions simply through lack of experience – from printing
up ranges that were too limited (most gift shops like to have
more than three or four designs on display) or in unpopular
formats (square), to producing cards that lacked commercial

Summary
Making Sense of the Marketplace

1.

Learning about the key areas in the creative industry is essential to deciding which sectors interest you most and who to approach for work.

2.

Internships with design groups, advertising agencies and magazines often pave the way to full-time jobs for designers; most illustrators are freelance, and generally get their first commissions from the editorial sector.

3.

Design groups differ in size and the services they provide for clients. They may be broad-based and/or multidisciplinary, or concentrate on specific sectors such as fashion or finance. Specializations vary widely, and include branding, packaging and web design.

4.

Advertising agencies pay the highest fees but you must be prepared to work hard – and to tight deadlines. Some specialize in specific media, such as print, television and film, online campaigns or direct mail.

5.

The editorial sector is wide ranging and includes magazines, newspapers, and trade and professional publications. Design and illustration styles vary according to readership, so it is important for practitioners to decide on the type of publication that best suits their abilities.

6.

Book publishing covers hardback and paperback fiction and non-fiction for children and adults. Many designers who later become freelance start off working in a publishing house, while children's picture books provide commissions for illustrators whose styles are suitable for this market.

7.

Comics and graphic novels are of interest to illustrators rather than designers. There are two routes into this sector: self-authoring independent comics and working for a commercial publisher on a freelance basis.

8.

Television and film are part of the entertainment industry, and as this is a niche market there is competition to work in these sectors. Software skills are important for designers who want to work in production houses. Freelance illustrators are regularly employed as storyboard and concept artists.

9.

Computer games development offers more opportunities for artists and animators than for designers – and is one of the few sectors that can provide illustrators with in-house or short-contract work. Artists should be familiar with screen resolutions and the file formats used in digital modelling.

10.

Greetings cards are part of the gift industry and can provide permanent employment for designers; roles can vary and some publishers prefer applicants with multiple skills. This creative area is one of the few where having a variety of illustrative styles is an advantage.

Long Island Graphic Design Agency.
Lyon, France
I learnt to work in a small team and
.... with colleagues. Book cover
.... work.

I try to be creative and to see things
differently to make my projects
interesting to me and to others.

ALIX
JEAMBRUN

Curriculum Vitae

12 Peoples Place
Warwick road
OX16 0FJ, Banbury, UK
O7544666516
alixjeambrun@gmail.com

Research and Cold-calling

3

Before you make overtures to organizations and individuals in the sectors of the creative industry that most interest you it is necessary to find out as much as possible about them. Understanding the precise nature of the work a specific company does, how you might best be of use to them, and the means by which they prefer to be approached will serve you infinitely better than contacting a broad range of vaguely possible employers. Target only those for whom your work is truly appropriate, and make sure whatever you send them as a visual appetizer honestly represents you as a practitioner and typifies the contents of your portfolio. Sometimes this may involve making individual promotional packages instead of, or in addition to, more general material you have already prepared. It may even necessitate producing a brand-new piece of work geared to a target's specific needs.

Opposite: Alix Jeambrun's beautifully rendered CV is both memorable and appropriate to her target market. It is representative of the type of work she aspires to – illustration and craft design.

Why Research
Is Important

The more you know about a potential employer before an interview, the more likely you are to make an impression. Regrettably, there is a certain breed of commissioner who takes active pleasure in causing the nervous first-time job seeker maximum discomfort so the better prepared you are, the more confident you will be. There are stories abound of art directors ripping up work or taking pleasure in dismissing you in the most soul-destroying manner – some industries, such as advertising, are renowned to be tougher than others. Or it is simply that there are some unpleasant characters out there, who take wicked advantage of their positions of power and influence, and you're likely to cross paths with a couple of them during your professional lifetime. Try to look upon these tiresome interludes as character building. The trick is to be able to recognize legitimate criticism, which usually goes something like this:

'I'd need to see specific examples of X/Y/Z before I can be sure you're absolutely right for us.'

'Your characters lack the distinctiveness and originality needed for the children's book market.'

'Your X is very strong but your Y needs further development.'

'There are too many illustrative styles here; I find it confusing.'

'Your work is probably better suited to the X sector than ours.'

'We don't really commission much X. Have you thought of approaching so-and-so instead?'

While opinions can be subjective, if the same criticism keeps recurring this is usually a reliable indicator that there is a genuine problem. The more aware you are of what an employer or commissioner is looking for, and the more confident you are in your ability to fulfil their criteria, the easier it is to appreciate and act on any valid criticism.

'It is always worth doing your homework and being honest with yourself about your style and who you target.'

Hazel Brown, Deputy Art Editor, *Radio Times*

The less focused you are when you target your work, the more likely you are to flounder on a tide of disparate feedback, none of it overly helpful. As a graphic design graduate desperate for her first full-time appointment, I once travelled miles to see a company I'd picked at random out of the only design directory available at the time. On my arrival, it became instantly apparent that it was rather more dedicated to industrial design – an area I had no talent for or, indeed, training in – than I had realized. My interviewer, no doubt as befuddled as I was as to what had brought me to the company, but feeling obliged to offer something in the way of professional advice, opined: 'I think you should remount everything in your folder on grey.' In retrospect, given that my work looked just fine mounted on black, this was surely as good an example of two-sided time wasting as any.

'Research the companies you like the work of. Not just the obvious ones. Find out who works in them and who gives out the jobs; his/her name (correct spelling) and a bit about them – their background; college, university. Send them a thoughtful, considered and personal professional letter/email, well laid out and signed. No "Dear anybody…" stock letters.'

Andy Ewan, Founding Partner, Ewan Searle Studio

Overleaf: Some pages from the online portfolio of New York-based Taiwanese cross-disciplinary practitioner, Tien-Min Liao (L) plus a self-promotional poster featuring a montage of her work, (R).

Targeting Your Research

As mentioned in chapter one, some art colleges offer more advice about professional practice than others – and, of course, there are also students who doggedly choose to inhabit their own little worlds until they graduate. Quite often I meet new practitioners who not only seem wholly unaware of the competition that abounds in every sphere, but also nurture ambitions that have little grounding in commercial reality. If you only work in black and white, you'll have fewer options than someone who works in colour; if you can't draw children, or characters per se, you'll have a limited career in children's books; and even if you're the world's foremost expert on Tolkien or the *Star Trek* franchise, this does not automatically mean your work is of the standard required to illustrate mass-market book covers.

Many similarly stark truths abound. Whether you are a designer or an illustrator, it's no use building castles in the air. An abundance of online and printed source material makes it relatively painless and straightforward to find suitable potential employers in the design world, while the ubiquitous and conspicuous nature of illustration makes it easy enough to research possible clients.

Jobs in the design world

As many junior designers are offered permanent employment by companies they did internships with as students, it's advisable to investigate the possibility of doing a placement while you're still in college. Focus is key; if you have a leaning towards a specialist area – branding in the retail sector, for example, or website design – investigate the possibility of doing an internship with a company that reflects your interest, though be aware that most student internships are unpaid. And, if you haven't yet thought that far ahead, start familiarizing yourself with the work of as many creative employers as possible. Even if you don't want to specialize you'll find tremendous variations in company ethos, clientele and approach to design in general. If, for instance, you're interested in working with illustrators or utilising your own illustrative skills as a designer, you need to know that some design groups commission next to no illustration at all and make sure you steer clear of them.

If you have reached the stage of researching potential employers to target, scanning job advertisements, even if you aren't qualified to apply for the positions being advertised, is invaluable. A company's size and geographical location, whether it is general or specialist in nature, the sectors it services, and how likely it is to hire people with multiple skills can be determined from an advertisement just as well as from a company website

or a profile in the creative press – though you're more likely to see examples of work and find contact names by assiduously scouring the latter. You may, in the rare instances you do stumble across an advertisement for a junior designer, find there are certain skills you need to hone or acquire in order to embark on your chosen path. If you're reading this while still a student, forewarned is forearmed: use whatever facilities are available to you while they're subsidized or free as further training can be expensive.

'I'm partly influenced by the design of a promo piece but more interested in contacting people who have shown samples of something of a similar nature to what we produce.'

Joy Monkhouse, freelance publishing designer, Scholastic

CONTACT

tienmin.l@gmail.com

917 498 6633

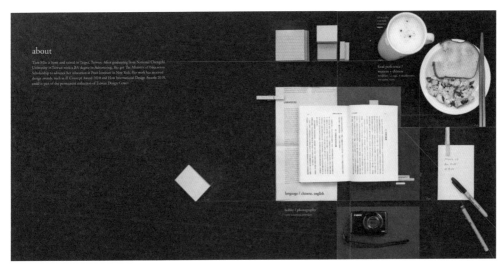

about

Tien-Min is born and raised in Taipei, Taiwan. After graduating from National Chengchi University in Taiwan with a BA degree in Advertising, She got The Ministry of Education Scholarship to advance her education at Pratt Institute in New York. Her work has received design awards, such as iF Concept Award 2010 and How International Design Awards 2010, and is part of the permanent collection of Taiwan Design Center.

mainland china 1,384 m ppl
taiwan 23 m ppl

mainland china 59:1 taiwan

population

"Ilha formosa"

rains

Alphabet

TARS

S

Visual design is just like a band performance. The guitarist, the bass player, the drummer, the vocalist, and the fiddler have to play their own parts excellently, and yet coordinate with the other performers, so they can perform to perfection. Besides the ability to portray different aspects of visual expression, it is important to understand how to balance each visual element, and then creating harmony.

'You get a lot of stuff you know you
won't commission in a million years.
Printed material has to be pretty special
for you to want to keep it. It only has
value if it's lovely.'

Mark Reddy, Head of Art, Bartle Bogle Hegarty

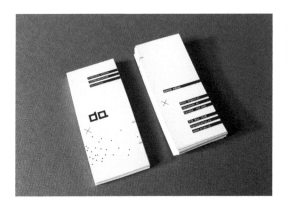

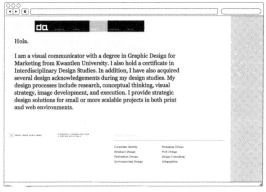

Opposite: Canadian freelance designer David Arias has created a 246-page book to function as his portfolio when visiting clients and design studios. Note how all additional forms of self-promotion echo the design of the book, creating a strong personal brand identity.

Below: Self-promotional material can give you an opportunity to exercise your creativity beyond the constraints of a commercial brief. These cards formed part of a collectable series, issued by Russell Cobb every 3–4 months over a 5-year period. In total, he produced 38 designs, which also enabled him to send complete mini-portfolios for clients to keep when requested.

Illustration commissioners

As mentioned in chapter two, the majority of freelance
illustrators tend to get their first commissions from editorial
clients. So, your first mission must be to familiarize yourself
with as wide a variety of magazines and newspapers as
possible (not just the ones you've heard of or happen to read
yourself; we're talking livelihood not lifestyle here), taking note
of the type of illustration they use if and where applicable. Ask
yourself whether the kind of work they favour bears any
similarity to yours; this could be a stylistic resemblance or have
more to do with subject matter or a certain way of thinking. If
you detect one or more similarities, congratulations; you've
found yourself a potential commissioner.

**'I work in children's books, and get
submissions of nudes, extreme violence
and adult editorial work all the time. I'd
say about 10–15 per cent is something
I might be able to use some day.'**

Steve Scott, Art Director, Scholastic

However, this applies only to illustrated editorial content.
When it comes to the advertisements, any illustrations therein
will have been commissioned not by the magazine but by
an advertising agency on behalf of whichever advertiser paid
to appear in the publication. If a magazine doesn't favour
illustrations or commissions work that bears no resemblance
to yours, move on. Publications that eschew illustrations usually
do so for a reason – which is unlikely to be a dearth of illustrators.
Some magazine editors simply do not care for illustrations or
feel they are inappropriate for their publication.

**'This happens with all illustrators, not just
newcomers. I receive samples of work
that is totally inappropriate for my company
very frequently.'**

Jonathan Christie, Art Director, Conran Octopus

A magazine's contents page gives the name of the person
responsible for commissioning – generally the art editor or art
director. Newspapers tend to be slightly less forthcoming in
this respect, though you will usually find the publisher's address
and telephone number listed somewhere in the publication. A
quick telephone call should provide you with the contact name
you need. Meanwhile, your own common sense will tell you
whether there are any subject-specific samples in your portfolio.
If there aren't, generate some fresh work as you'll need it
to convince the commissioner you're a suitable illustrator for
the publication.

Be prepared to find an audience in areas you haven't
previously considered and embrace new content should the
necessity arise. You may, for example, be interested in
narrative work but find relatively few publications that feature
illustrated short stories. A medical or psychiatric journal, or a
magazine geared towards social workers, may run illustrated
case histories and, from an illustrator's point of view, these can
be treated as narratives. When searching for new clients, an
open mind will always stand you in good stead.

**'I have a reasonably good knowledge
of design – type, layout, etc. – but I'm
mostly doing illustration. But it helps a lot.
I write my children's books and do the
layout and general packaging. I think the
graphics background makes me a better
illustrator and it can help when talking
with designer clients.'**

Ian Bilbey, freelance illustrator

Below: UK publication, *Creative Review* (shown here with an illustrated cover by Billie Jean), is just one of many highly informative industry magazines showcasing creative talent. Most art school libraries subscribe to these on a regular basis as do some public libraries.

Research Resources

There's no excuse for not being industry-savvy these days – though, granted, there's such an abundance of easily accessible reference material it can sometimes be difficult to know where to start. There is a comprehensive listings section at the end of this book but here, in the meantime, is a brief rundown of some of the resources you can draw on.

'I find that when you apply for the wrong job no good will come of it, you're just wasting time. Applying for bad jobs is like going out on dates with people you don't like. There's little point in the long run, and it'll just distract you from your true goals.'

Josh Keay, freelance designer

Professional journals

Numerous weekly, monthly and bimonthly titles devoted to the creative industry are available in print or online. Within them you will find profiles of companies and individual practitioners as well as job advertisements. You will also find articles on industry trends plus updates on clients, company mergers and takeovers, and the promotions and relocations of various movers and shakers. Even magazines aimed at hobbyists and aspiring practitioners can be worth a look as they frequently offer all kinds of pointers from industry professionals.

Annuals and sourcebooks

Glossy, large-format annuals and sourcebooks celebrating design, advertising, illustration, photography and multimedia abound. Some accompany competitions, with featured entries nominated by elected panels of industry professionals. (Always check the judges, as some are less well known – and therefore less often approached by aspiring newcomers – than those who regularly feature in the creative press.) Others are simply directories that showcase the work of practitioners, organizations that represent practitioners, or both; these can offer insights into the kinds of client, projects and practitioners with which potential commissioners are involved. Illustrators seeking representation can get a realistic overview of how agencies differ. Both types of publication tend to have free distribution among commissioners and employers, and are either archived online or have affiliated websites.

'Graphic design positions are placed in our own titles, *Design Week* and *Creative Review*.'

Colin McHenry, Group Art Director, Centaur Media

'(We advertise) on our website; through
selected schools and the AIGA website.'

Christopher Pullman, Vice President, Design (Public Television) USA

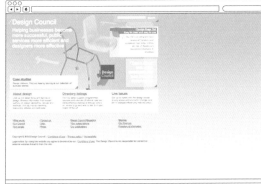

Yearbooks, mailing lists and industry directories

There are several yearbooks and associated online resources devoted to specific markets such as publishing, advertising, computer games and the film and television industry. It's also possible to purchase reasonably priced databases and mailing lists of creative organizations of all kinds from marketing resource specialists. These tend to be sector specific, and are updated frequently and include contact details. However, a more general overview can be acquired courtesy of various creative industry directories. These can often be found in specialist libraries, though many of their listings can be accessed free online.

Libraries

For those strapped for cash, yearbooks, directories and industry magazines can sometimes be found in the reference section of public libraries, especially if there's an art college in the vicinity; or try art college libraries – remember, though, that different campuses may not necessarily carry the same publications. Enterprising illustrators in search of more unusual editorial titles may benefit from stalking the aisles of university libraries, as the magazines they archive reflect the subjects taught.

Industry-related websites, portals and blogs

If you want to know who an advertising agency's clients are, see if a design group specializes in brand identity or exhibition graphics, or find out if a publisher favours illustrations on its book jackets, the company website should be your first port of call. Not only will you get an overall idea of the organization's output, you could well find job advertisements, calls for speculative submissions or information related to internships.

Industry bodies and organizations with a professional membership also have websites and use them to promote publications, job opportunities and various events, such as competitions, seminars, conferences and exhibitions. Some offer subscribers the facility to promote their work online, while those that host discussion forums provide members with the means to network and share their professional experience.

Of course, anyone with a basic grasp of the Internet and access to a web-hosting site can call themselves an industry spokesperson. However, quality control does exist. Selective,

multi-authored or invitation-only design and illustration blogs are great places to start when checking out the competition – and you should find some decent links, too. Individual blogs can also be used for research purposes, since practitioners frequently post information on who is currently hiring them.

Lastly, there is a plethora of widely differing communities and online directories that deal with creative jobs of all kinds. Some are set up for love and moderated by practitioners. Others are set up for money by specialized recruitment agencies, industry magazines, national newspapers or portfolio-hosting companies. Most of these are free to employers and commissioners, with practitioners paying to upload online CVs or portfolios. Some provide discussion forums as well as career tips or links to industry-related blogs and articles in the creative press. The directories, in particular, can be invaluable as they offer the facility to search for creative employers according to discipline and geographical location.

'All our juniors come via work placements, people who either keep in touch or make themselves indispensable while they're here. We do see designers who approach us speculatively. If we like a PDF or website, we'll call someone in. We never advertise.'

Rob Howsam, Creative Director, Purpose Design

Cold-calling

Despite the increasing popularity of emails and Internet resources I'm a great believer in the value of face-to-face meetings and entreat you – particularly in the case of speculative applications and regardless of your discipline – to make securing one your objective wherever geographically practicable. While the organizations and individuals you target will usually keep any well-designed, imaginative promotional material you have sent them on file, impressing them with further examples of your brilliance while their interest is piqued will ensure your work stays uppermost in their mind for longer. This means getting on the phone and following up any overtures you make to a possible employer, no matter how shy or uncomfortable you feel.

In the face of extreme competition, sending out a handful of mailers then sitting back and waiting for dream-job offers to come rolling in is neither an effective nor a realistic option. For illustrators in particular, being proactive is crucial as many commissioners have a rapid turnover of illustrations and their needs can therefore vary on an ongoing basis. A good start is to Google the names of art editors/directors who have judged illustration competitions.

'Those who phone have 95 per cent done their homework. Those who email are 75 per cent relevant. Post is worst; at least 60 per cent is inappropriate.'

Martin Colyer, Art Director, *Reader's Digest*

Whether you are a graphic designer or an illustrator, one of the most frustrating aspects of cold-calling is to be told that a company or individual has no need of your services as they already have a pool of stalwarts they've been drawing on for years. In many areas of creative employment, the digital revolution has significantly depleted the size of the average art department. With fewer designers carrying what used to be the workload of many, time is at a premium and, for commissioners, risk-taking is consequently less appealing; it's easy to appreciate why falling back on practitioners they already know appeals to them. Yet, given the nature of their profession, they need to be on top of prevailing trends, so your striving to become a known quantity could, if you are successful, ultimately benefit them. It's easy to overlook this fact at the beginning of your career when confidence can waiver because of the risk of appearing pushy. Polite persistence – as necessary an attribute as a winning portfolio – is the answer here.

There's also a good chance that your interpersonal skills will play a significant part in winning an employer's or commissioner's confidence. Examples of your work alone won't enable him or her to determine how swift, reliable or adaptable you might be, or how well the two of you would work together.

A creative director of my acquaintance called in a recent design graduate on the basis of some particularly engaging samples – only to meet with an aggressive individual so firmly convinced of their own greatness that, professional inexperience notwithstanding, they felt a junior position to be beneath them. While such chutzpah and fierce self-belief might have gone down well elsewhere, in the context of a smallish, close-knit design team that shared the same workspace, it was perceived as a lack of humility that could generate ill-feeling. I have had illustrators turn up for meetings anything up to 40 minutes late, on completely the wrong day, or in various altered states of consciousness. I've also encountered arrogance, near-monosyllabic nonchalance and a complete inability to take constructive criticism with anything approaching good grace – not ideal if you're hoping to work with or for the person giving you professional feedback. While talent is paramount, when it comes to attitude and personal chemistry a working relationship is no different from any other kind.

'We would avoid someone who was emulating what they considered "Airside style". We want designers with their own thoughts and styles so that they bring something to the pot.'

Anne Brassier, PR and New Business, Airside

Speculative Applications

Given that full-time employment is commonplace for graphic designers, many graduates assume they'll be responding to specific job advertisements and attending formal interviews rather than going the speculative route more commonly associated with a freelance career in illustration. However, junior vacancies aren't necessarily advertised and even those that are often specify a minimum of 1–2 years experience. Some designers come by their first job as a result of doing an internship, or even a succession of internships, but many do so simply by being in the right place at the right time – and, for this to happen, you need to make connections in the industry. So, unless you're one of the privileged few who are offered a full-time position during or following a college placement, there's every likelihood you'll be making speculative applications.

'My pet peeve is young designers who cold-call me on the phone and ask only, "Are you hiring?" I will almost always take the time to review the portfolio of a young designer who approaches me in a respectful, candid, thorough manner. But I will never – no matter how hungry I am for new talent – answer "Are you hiring?" with "Yes".'

Doug Powell, Creative Director, Schwartz Powell Design

Whether you are a designer or an illustrator, securing so much as a ten-minute meeting with a time-poor art director/editor besieged on all sides by graduates frantic to pay off their student loans is a hard enough task even when you have done your homework. And, if the person concerned heads up a hip, flavour-of-the-month organization that everybody else also wants to work for, it's likely to be even harder. The common response to this age-old predicament is to fire off unfocused begging letters to every potential employer or commissioner within a 100-mile radius in the hope of making a random strike. While understandable, this is not recommended. The postage costs involved can be prohibitive and if you're essentially targeting large numbers of the wrong people the frustration factor is likely to be high.

Emails may save money, but it is easy for the intended recipients to mislay or overlook unsolicited ones, or swear blind they never received them in the first place. The emails often get no further than the company spam filter, while even those that do get through may irk; no one likes a digital file that takes forever to download. Besides, art directors/editors are capricious and sensitive when it comes to the samples they receive. Some swear by digital media, others have an avowed preference for print. Many happily paper the walls of their workplace with promotional paraphernalia, while others consider a bare, minimalist environment integral to the creative process and work that doesn't immediately appeal to them goes straight into the bin. About the only thing they agree on is that they don't like having their time wasted. The less relevant the samples an art director/editor receives, the more likely they are to jettison them and the less likely you are to receive any constructive feedback. Sending misleading examples could result in an interview – but one that elicits negative feedback. Either way, not great for morale when you are trying to launch your career.

'I receive many speculative calls and emails, and posted samples in all shapes and sizes. Many of these I think are inappropriate for the magazine. I also receive calls from illustrators who have researched little about the magazine and are often unaware of the postal address. I do expect people to do the groundwork and be aware of the magazine's illustration styles and content.'

Alison Lawn, Art Director, New Scientist

Below: Categories in the prestigious V&A Illustration Awards include Best Illustrated Book, Book Cover, Editorial Illustration and Student Illustrator of the Year. The work is subsequently featured in the museum's annual exhibition, while all entries can be viewed online. Seen here are two pieces by 2011 winner, Michael Redmond, from the Royal College of Art; *Before The Dive* (left) and *Fruits* (right).

Student Exhibitions and Competitions

Many creative employers attend student degree exhibitions, such as 'New Designers' and the D&AD's 'New Blood' in the United Kingdom, and events organized by the Art Directors Club in the United States and by the Australian Graphic Design Association. With this in mind, remember that on this kind of occasion potential employers or clients will be researching you, rather than you them. Try not to stray too far from your stand on opening night, and make sure you provide a visitors' book and plenty of promotional material for interested parties to take away. Finally, entering student design competitions can help to raise your profile substantially, so enter them if and when you have the opportunity. Remember: the more professional contacts you make, the greater your chances of finding work in the long run.

'We don't advertise for junior designers. We keep all CVs of interest that are sent to us or ask designers we know already. We also attend graduation shows and "New Designers".

Anne Brassier, PR and New Business, Airside

Summary
Research
and Cold-calling

1.

Finding out about the organizations and individuals in your chosen sector of the creative industry will enable you to target only those for whom your work is appropriate.

2.

Sources of information include professional journals, sourcebooks, annuals, and mailing lists and industry directories. There are also resources such as websites, portals and blogs, and online communities and directories that specialize in creative jobs in a variety of disciplines.

3.

Securing a face-to-face meeting with a potential employer or commissioner should be one of your main objectives. Once you have sent them any kind of promotional material it is essential to telephone them and ask whether you can show them your portfolio.

4.

Interpersonal skills can be significant during a presentation: a potential employer or commissioner needs to determine whether they could have a good working relationship with you, and how reliable or adaptable you are.

5.

Be focused when you make speculative applications. Art editors/directors don't like having their time wasted, so make sure any samples you send to an organization are relevant to its requirements.

6.

Competitions and student degree exhibitions can help to raise your profile so far as creative employers are concerned; and in the case of the latter, they will be researching you, rather than you them.

Art Director: Matt Bolton
Designer: Matt Bolton
Editor: Matt Bolton
Writer: Matt Bolton

London College of Communication
FdA Graphic Design for Communication

STRAIGHT FROM THE HORSES MOUTH

Creating a
Good Portfolio

4

At the risk of stating the obvious, a good portfolio – whether it be print or digital – is one that lands the type of job or commission you're looking for. Your portfolio is the means by which potential employers or commissioners will familiarize themselves with your work. It should, therefore, adequately showcase your skills without boring your target to death or, conversely, giving them short shrift.

Opposite: Graphic designer Matt Bolton amply demonstrates how to make a powerful visual impression at the start (top) and finish (bottom) of a print portfolio.

Basic Approaches

I was once consulted by an established botanical illustrator. The work was of a consistently high standard, covered a wide variety of botanical subject matter, in a variety of media, from both a decorative and informational standpoint. However, I was forced to look through no less than five portfolios in order to determine this – which took up a hefty chunk of our allocated 60 minutes. I lost the will to live halfway through a succession of unbound, black-and-white, scarcely distinguishable garden plans – which I counted, since by this time it was my only means of staying awake; there were almost 40. No commissioner needs that much convincing somebody can draw a water feature. The illustrator in question could have been saved the ignominy of fetching up in this book as a cautionary tale by some judicious pruning – for instance, three plans, maybe one in colour, featuring three discernibly different types of garden design. Point made more than adequately in less than a minute; and on to the next section of the portfolio.

'I once heard that one's own work should be good enough to be housed in a paper bag. I have to agree with that. A nice presentation is helpful – as long as the work doesn't suffer for the presentation.'
Kristina DiMatteo, Art Director, *Print*

You're not a student any more; there's no need to show every project you've ever worked on in order to impress or show your dedication. For maximum effectiveness your portfolio should simply demonstrate how you are at your best as a practitioner, and how well you understand the needs of the commissioner who is looking at your work. Moreover, it should do so quickly since most introductory presentations don't last anything like an hour; truth be told, you will be lucky if you get 15 minutes. (And as for 15 uninterrupted minutes…) This is especially pertinent to illustrators making speculative approaches to commissioners rather than to designers attending formal interviews for full-time positions. And, while it is imperative that you are able to talk potential employers through the contents of your folder articulately and in depth, your core strengths should also be apparent in your absence. With time at a premium, portfolio drop-offs are the norm for many organizations, as they allow employers to view work in their own time with the added option of showing it to colleagues who might not be available

for a presentation. Illustration agencies often also favour this approach as they tend to be small organizations and are frequently targeted by artists whose work is unsuitable.

'I always think simplicity is the best option. I think it is the work which should shine, not necessarily the style of presentation.'
Alison Lawn, Art Director, *New Scientist*

Should you be asked to drop off a print portfolio for a couple of hours – or even a couple of days – don't panic any more than you would if you were asked to email a client some jpegs or a PDF of your work. No reputable company would dream of ripping off your work or publishing your images without your consent; not least because the odds against you finding out and suing them are slim. Likewise, don't despair at the brevity of your presentation should you be fortunate enough to be granted a face-to-face meeting. Anyone who's been in the creative industries long enough to attain a senior position can not only zip through a portfolio in minutes, they can also fully take in the contents. 'Visual communication' is what they do for a living. Plus, it doesn't take all that long to answer the question: 'Is this person good enough to work for me?'

'If a student or designer has work in the portfolio, it should be their work and they should be able to talk about whatever role they played in it. If it was designed by a senior designer and they helped with the final, that's OK, just be honest about your role.'
Robert Linsky, Senior Vice President of Design, Art Plus Technology

Learn to be Objective

Being able to take stock of your creative strengths and weaknesses is every bit as important as understanding the needs of your chosen target. Commissioners, employers and even practitioners have different opinions when it comes to what to include in a portfolio – but it's generally agreed you should start with your strongest piece and end on a similarly high note. Since it's a fact of creative life that few practitioners are – or remain – 100 per cent happy with what they produce, I recommend aiming for around 87 per cent satisfaction with whatever you choose to start with – and, for that matter, with everything that follows. While I believe this to be both realistic and achievable, I also understand it can be easier said than done, especially for anyone who is just starting out.

'A professional portfolio should contain final printed samples of their best work, and should show pieces appropriate for the job they are seeking. If anyone includes pieces that are not great, I am unlikely to use them. I would rather see a book with only a few really good pieces, than one with a lot of inconsistent pieces.'

Steve Scott, Art Director, Scholastic

Although students generally receive regular, constructive criticism while developing their skills, the feedback from tutors and peers can sometimes be wildly conflicting and, on occasion, biased, so it's hardly surprising that some of designers and illustrators emerge from art college confused and unsure of themselves. However, since industry professionals are likely to have similarly diverse reactions to the work they see, your portfolio is destined to be a mess if you don't learn to value your own judgement. I've had many new graduates confess mid-consultation, 'So-and-so told me this was my strongest piece of work but I never really liked it.' In most instances, the decision to include a sample you're not sure about can be born of panic, as in: 'But what if it's the piece that might get me the job?' But, frankly, what if it is? If, deep down, you suspect the work is bad, or the thought of having to repeat the exercise is profoundly unappealing, would you really want the job it got you? Since it's as impossible to sell work you've no confidence in as it is to be all things to everyone you meet professionally, you will always be best served by being true to yourself.

Bad work will stick in the viewer's mind, whether it's irrelevant, derivative, repetitive, overly self-indulgent, out of date (it's not unheard of for people to show pieces that are 15 or 20 years old; one illustrator showed me a drawing he'd done at the age of six, as testament to his lifelong genius) or simply not up to the same standard as the rest of your work. Showcasing the last, in particular, will suggest you can't tell your good, sound pieces from those that are not so good – which can make it difficult for a commissioner to put their faith in you. Think of it from their point of view: why risk using someone whose work is plainly inconsistent when there are plenty of other practitioners they can choose from?

'Seeing work of varying standards in the same portfolio would put me off commissioning someone.'

Anamaria Stanley, Art Director, TimeOut

The Contents

As covered in the following chapter, a portfolio can take several forms but format aside, when it comes to the contents of yours, the same factors should always be taken into consideration. With an abundance of keen up-and-coming talent at their disposal, potential employers and commissioners will take the contents of your portfolio at face value. If a sample is given pride of place they'll conclude you are ready, willing and able to produce more pieces in the same vein; and, by the same token, if you show only good, consistent work, they will take your reliability as read. But if certain skills are conspicuous by their absence they'll assume you don't have them or are reluctant to exercise them. In order to decide which pieces to include in your portfolio you will need to ask yourself some serious questions. I suggest you start with the following:

Are all the pieces up to my highest standards?

It's always more effective to show a small, well-edited selection of your strongest work than reams of mediocre fillers. Take a good, hard look at the current contents of your portfolio and remove anything that falls into any of the following categories:

Work you think is weak. People will ask you to talk about the samples in your portfolio. Anything you might feel tempted to make excuses for should not be on display; ditto anything you know another practitioner could do ten times better than you. If you don't believe in it, bin it.

Work that's misleading. This includes one-off experimental pieces you're not sure you could replicate; college exercises that failed to engage you; jobs you took on purely because someone was crazy/desperate enough to pay you to do them; or illustrative styles you no longer enjoy doing or, worse still, never did enjoy doing. While it's true that published work and a broad range of skills impress potential employers, it's no good showing anything that's wholly unrepresentative of who you are or the kind of work you want to do. They'll only assume you want to do more of it. Start as you mean to go on.

Work you can't deliver. Rather than designers, this tends to affect illustrators. For example, in order to produce images similar to those in their portfolio some may require equipment to which they no longer have access. An ex-tutor may have promised an artist that he or she could use the college printmaking facilities any time they wanted to, but clients need jobs done at weekends and over the summer break. And it's no use showing a piece of work that took ten times longer to

do than the average client's deadline. The simple fact is that showing a technique you can't replicate will do your professional credibility no good whatsoever. Investigate renting or sharing a printmaking studio; find a way to speed up the way you work; but don't waste time and money selling a service or product you can't guarantee.

'Any kind of sloppiness in the craft of the portfolio is unacceptable.'

Jennifer Pastore, Associate Photo Editor, *T: The New York Times Style Magazine*

Is self-indulgent work taking up prime portfolio space?

While employers and commissioners seek originality of thought, and while personal projects are ideal for conveying your creative individuality, your work needs to be accessible in order to get you hired. To some extent an element of self-indulgence is unavoidable, especially if you've only just left college. You have, after all, probably spent the last few months working flat-out on a couple of self-directed, final major projects. If you are a designer you have, with any luck, been engaged in the area(s) of design in which you are most interested in gaining employment. The same, regrettably, cannot always be said of illustrators.

Rough, half-finished observational drawings ripped out of sketchbooks and featuring a) your grandma, b) your pet, c) random people in cafés, or d) jazz musicians are not illustration and, like academic life-studies, have no business taking up valuable portfolio space. Most clients take it for granted that an illustrator knows how to draw. The only scenario in which that sketch of your grandma is likely to prove of any commercial benefit is if you have a meeting with an art director/editor who is commissioning illustrations for a brochure promoting a care home for the elderly. Then – and only then – should you include it as part of a professional body of work.

Commerciality is about producing work that is relevant to the marketplace. If you want to eat this week rather than some time next month, you need to find common ground between what you enjoy doing and what your client actually needs, especially if you're not the only illustrator on the block.

A problem with self-directed, final major projects, that can affect both designers and illustrators, is that they may dominate a portfolio. If a project has some commercial relevance, this can

'A chap, in order to display his photographic /film skills acquired while at university, put in some stills of a film he had made – a kind of horror film with him and another student slashed to death (with lots of mock blood, naked, on the floor of a public toilet). Although very well "executed" this certainly left a lasting impression.'

Joy Monkhouse, freelance publishing designer, Scholastic

be a good, solid foundation on which to build. However, if it is self-indulgent and difficult for clients to relate to in a commercial sense, you will in all probability have to create a new one. Securing an interview is tough enough in itself. If you fail to impress the first time around you may never get another chance. For example, an illustrator I know attended an interview with a client, an art director, he was desperate to work for. The client professed to like a piece he had entered for a national competition and asked him about the idea behind it. When he was halfway through answering the question, the client told him there were too many ideas informing the piece and, consequently, he'd gone off it. The illustrator, who was modest and well-mannered, accepted this criticism, and said he intended to learn by it and that he hoped to return at some future date with an improved portfolio. The client replied that he didn't allow second chances – it sounds harsh but he is nonetheless representative of the kind of commissioner you may encounter.

'I have seen portfolios with no direction; the person was not sure what area he/she wanted to specialize in.'

John Oakey, Art Director, *TimeOut* Group

What new samples should I add to my portfolio?

Once you have painstakingly researched the output and needs of your market and chosen employer you will need to ask yourself whether you've covered all bases adequately. Designers who are looking for full-time jobs in a specialized sector need to demonstrate their passion for, and commitment to, that field. Advertising agencies want to see advertisements; book publishers want to see books, and so on.

It is also necessary to demonstrate versatility in your chosen sector. Show the advertising agency how you would approach campaigns for different products and services; provide ideas for press advertisements, direct mail and digital marketing, apps, posters, virals and television campaigns (in the case of the last, storyboards are acceptable to most art directors and some prefer them). If an agency concentrates on a particular sector, such as the travel industry or the motor trade, ensure you have at least one campaign that addresses its area of expertise. Likewise, show a book publisher cover designs that span a variety of genres; also give them double-

page spreads if and where applicable; and consider promotional posters. Strive to reflect an understanding of the readership the company targets and an appreciation of the kind of literature they publish. You may need to build up a broad body of work in your chosen area and choose which pieces to put in – or take out of – your portfolio, depending on who you are going to see. The same goes for freelance designers approaching a variety of clients. A portfolio is rarely 'done' for the duration; any more than your website would be. As a creative practitioner, you are a constant work in progress, evolving and exploring new avenues and platforms for your skills; your portfolio should be a reflection of this.

For less specialized designers, especially those approaching broad-based or multidisciplinary consultancies, it is vital that their portfolio not only shows that they have the skills to solve a diverse range of design problems but also that it demonstrates consistency of vision. If, for instance, you've designed a corporate identity for a restaurant chain you may want to show how it works beyond the standard letterhead. You could show how the colour scheme you've chosen can be used in the interiors of the restaurants or how the logo could work on their exteriors; you could suggest how the company website might look; or, envisaging a time when the chain decides to market its own food products, design packaging for them. If, on the other hand, you are applying to a less broad-based design organization – one that specializes mainly in design for the web, for example, or packaging – you should concentrate on showing versatility across that particular discipline.

'It's important to see the realities of work created professionally. How someone solves problems for a client is very different than for themselves.'

Kristina DiMatteo, Art Director, *Print*

Should new samples be put in context?

For designers, their work is the context, and images might theoretically be placed within it. So far as cross-disciplinary practitioners are concerned, using their own illustrations or photographs in a layout they've designed is unlikely to present a problem to the majority of clients or creative employers. However, if you are applying for a design position, it can work against you if the design element in your portfolio is significantly

Ernest Morris

Graphic Design & Typography

+44(0)7823 886020
motionweb@hotmail.com

Brief: Create an identity for a new museum based in Vienna and Typography.

Info: The museum is including elements such as a product brochure, the museum's positioning statement and stationery, a website and a brand.

Response: A branding for a museum of Type opening in 2009. The creation of the museum came about as a collaborative work that has been conceived as being museum dedicated to type. The identity reflects the contrast between both the weightiness of design in which the primaries were running and stating that with contemporary design at the end that the museum is now placed.

Print Portfolio

BD Student Best – December 2008

Type Factory

Ernest Morris

Graphic Design & Typography

+44(0)7823 886020
motionweb@hotmail.com

Brief: Create a fanzine that can be produced and sold. The aim of the project is to make a financially viable piece of design. Essentially cover the costs of production and also... try to make a profit.

Info: Screen printed t-shirts, posters and covers of the fanzine and inside a combination of typography, photography and illustration. Collaborative project.

Response: We chose to produce a fanzine that fought typographic and design related ideas as well as celebrating popular pieces of design of the moment. Each fanzine came with a free t-shirt and also had free details so that the t-shirts could be bought off the wards on their own.

Print Portfolio

University Project – April 2009

Typographic T-Shirts

overshadowed by the amount of illustration or photography, especially in an environment, such as editorial design, where roles can be strictly defined. For illustrators, however, one of the easiest ways to persuade a commissioner of their eminent usability is to place their work in the context of an existing design.

Given that most illustrators receive their first commissions from editorial clients, the ubiquitous mock-up – replacing the illustrations in a published magazine article with your own images, usually digitally – places your work in a context potential clients can relate to. In addition, producing mock-ups can be a valuable learning experience. If you've never done one before, it's remarkably similar to doing an actual job: having to generate ideas in response to a text that might be less than inspiring; working to a specified size or format; even running the gamut of unsympathetic typography and/or printing that bears little resemblance to the colours in your illustrations. And seeing your work reduced (often greatly, in practice) may also make you think about the quality of its line, the effectiveness of the media you used and the complexity of the images. Be assured that mock-ups are legitimate since you're not attempting to pass off another illustrator's work as your own or vice versa.

If you are an illustrator with strong, assured design skills there is nothing to stop you redesigning an editorial layout to your own liking. (And, if you are more oriented to book publishing, there's definitely nothing to stop you mocking up a book jacket, especially if hand-rendered type is a feature of your work.) However, while most commissioners don't have a problem with mock-ups per se, those who do usually cite poor design as the reason. If design isn't your strong point, simply use what is already there. If you can't find a layout you like in the magazine you're targeting, simply choose one from a similar publication that will do better justice to your work.

Some further considerations for mock-ups include:

Opt for layouts that are simply designed, rather than cramped.

Choose layouts where the image you are replacing is large enough to do proper justice to your work.

Always use the article you illustrated, as opposed to an unrelated one whose layout you prefer: inserting a drawing that illustrates the vagaries of the international stock market next to a recipe for summer pudding won't work.

Display only your amended version of the layout, not the original illustration next to yours.

Avoid old, dusty mock-ups that no longer look up to scratch. If an old idea was great, rework it.

Try to avoid displaying your mock-ups followed or preceded by a larger version of the same artwork. While this can be done in a special case, if used throughout it can be repetitious.

In the absence of mock-ups, published samples or photographs of work in situ, I suggest that both designers and illustrators should use captions. These must be legible, concise and consistent in style; they should also be discreet as they shouldn't dominate the content of your work.

'I'd rather see the work alone than a mock-up. Students often choose to illustrate stories where for me it would have been better to use a photograph. I can find that distracts from the work.'

Alison Lawn, Art Director, *New Scientist*

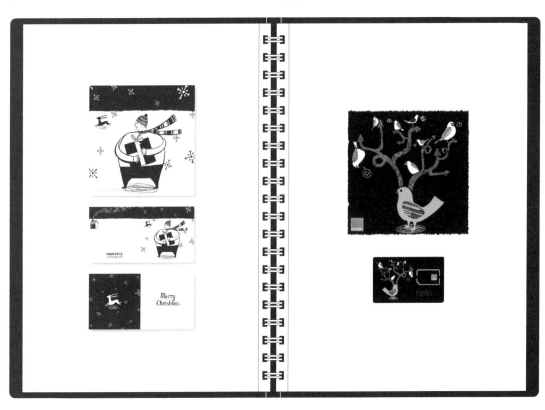

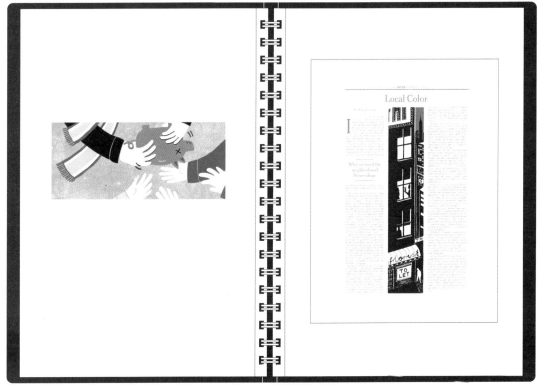

How many samples should I include?

It's my firm belief that the number of samples that are included
in a portfolio is down to the practitioner's discretion and
common sense: there is no right, one-size-fits-all answer. Some
art editors/directors opine that prospective employees should
have no more than 3–6 projects in their portfolios. This is
probably fine for designers who want a career in branding, but
is scarcely enough to show their full range if they want to design
book jackets. Similarly, an illustrator of children's picture books
who specializes in animals, with a complex style heavy on
intricate decorative detail, will require significantly fewer samples
to make his or her point than a cartoonist with a simple, linear
style and a broader potential client base.

It is important to remember, though, that nothing should
be left to chance. If you are the children's book illustrator who
specializes in animals, and your samples mainly feature dogs
and cats, commissioners who are well served for artists will
assume you can't draw guinea pigs or zebras. Don't expect
potential employers to be mind-readers; some of them will
require you to spell out the obvious.

**'At the end of the day it's always about
the quality and relevance of the work.'**

Dave Day, Art Director, Fallon

How do I show published work?

Most creative employers will be delighted and reassured to
see published work in your portfolio, so give it pride of place.
Job advertisements for junior designers often stipulate some
professional experience – which can be disheartening – but
you don't necessarily need to have worked in-house for a
year. Freelance work also counts. This includes jobs you've
done for relatives or friends; live briefs you did at college or
projects worked on during internships. Providing the work is
representative and up to the required standard, it can be an
effective stepping stone to gaining full-time employment or
further freelance commissions. Your interviewer won't know
you designed that logo for your brother's friend's record label
or your cousin's coffee shop; to them it's simply evidence
that someone was prepared to take a chance on you, and
you delivered.

At college it's customary for students to show work in
chronological order, building up to their latest and best
project. However, in the context of a real-world presentation this
is not the way to go. If a potential employer or commissioner
has to wade through endless examples of college work, you
may have lost their attention by the time they reach the jewel in
your creative crown – so put your published work as near to the
front of your portfolio as possible. For an interviewer who is
cautious about placing their trust in a novice, it marks you out
as a professional from the start, and hopefully makes the
presentation more relaxed for both of you.

Most illustration commissioners like to see work in its
printed context, as this can easily show their colleagues or clients
how they might use you. However, when it comes to advertising
art directors it's best to show your images in isolation. This is
because comissioners in agencies can be highly critical of their
rivals' campaigns and, in some cases, this can prejudice them
against using an illustrator or photographer. Some artists
overcome this problem by displaying additional reduced images
in their published context as an addendum; however, I
wouldn't recommend this unless you want to work only for
advertising agencies.

**'Junior art directors or, in our case, art
editors, would need to show a breadth and
depth of work. They must be able to
handle typography confidently. This is very
important. An attention to detail and some
wit in their design. They will need to show
that they can commission photographers
and illustrators.'**

Colin McHenry, Group Art Director, Centaur Media

Below: Including sketchbooks as
an optional extra in your portfolio can be
beneficial, especially if like Russell Cobb
(bottom) these are highly personalized. If,
however, you prefer to travel light, why not
take a leaf out of Shaun Doyle's portfolio
(top) and mount up a small cross-section
of sketchbook work instead.

'I like sketches and notebooks.
However, it is the end result which
is of importance.'

Alison Lawn, Art Director, *New Scientist*

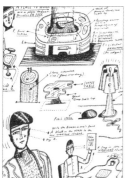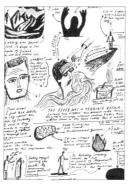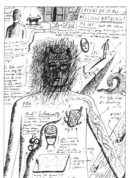

Overleaf: Janine Rewell is a freelance cross-disciplinary practitioner based in Helsinki. To keep things simple for her clients, her online portfolio is divided into separate sections for graphic design (top) and illustration (bottom).

How Many Portfolios?

Should I include my sketchbooks?

In a word, yes. However, not all employers and commissioners are in agreement about how useful sketchbooks are, and even those who are interested in your creative process are liable to get bored if they are forced to look at too many.

'Sketchbooks are really fun to look at, but certainly not enough for me to hire someone.'

Steve Scott, Art Director, Scholastic

I recommend that both designers and illustrators include one or two sketchbooks as an optional extra should a commissioner wish to have a look at them at the end of a presentation. In addition, so far as designers are concerned, some commissioners are not averse to seeing working roughs and initial ideas alongside finished projects. However, I would urge a degree of caution. Don't include developmental work for all your projects; concentrate instead on just one, or those that show your creative thinking at its absolute best. Too many roughs could make you seem unfocused and detract from the overall impact of your work.

'I like to see the workings of the mind. Not too much, but enough to show reportage sketches, idea development or just how a finished image came to be.'

Jonathan Christie, Art Director, Conran Octopus

Because there are several different ways of presenting work, you will inevitably end up with several. Full-size or scaled-down print portfolios for drop-offs; PDFs to send digitally; print portfolios, laptops or tablet devices for face-to-face presentations, or a combination of these. A designer who is working in print and digital media may choose to develop a print portfolio to show to clients alongside a laptop presentation of their digital work – as might a multi-disciplinary practitioner, such as an illustrator with animation skills. Whether you are a designer, illustrator or cross-disciplinary practitioner, you may well have a case for putting together more than one portfolio – though an alternative is to divide a single portfolio into sections dedicated to specific disciplines or styles. The aim is to confuse people as little as possible.

It is generally best for an illustrator who has vastly differing styles that appeal to separate markets (biting political satire and picture books for the under-fives, for example) to put together separate portfolios. Where the lines of demarcation are not obvious, it is possible to incorporate several styles in one portfolio, but care must be taken to ensure that the images flow in some sort of logical order. Work can be grouped according to subject matter, medium, mood, for example, but, given that you'll have limited time in which to make a lasting impression on your interviewer, it's vital that the portfolio reads as a cohesive whole. A jumble of random images that bear little relation to each other is unlikely to be remembered as anything other than a mess – and the chances are it won't even be remembered.

Designers and illustrators who approach a number of companies on a speculative basis may have two portfolios: one suitable for drop-offs and another for face-to-face presentations. Cross-disciplinary practitioners may choose to have different portfolios that show skills that are specific to various kinds of job – or to the requirements of a client who may be less than open-minded towards a portfolio that reveals them in all their multi-skilled glory. Lastly, illustrators who opt for agency representation may be required to put together more than one portfolio, especially if their work covers several fields or if the agent has offices abroad.

JA/
NINE
RE/
WELL

PACKAGING MUSIC
Design for a cd package and a booklet.
2008 /// RISD

Graphic Design

  Tuli & Savu

  Packaging music

  Christmas Greetings

  Mandala

  Smiles for miles

  Escape Diary

  Nolla magazine

  Geopool

  Relative directions

  Spork package

  Font

  Attention book

  Price of Beauty

Illustration

About

JA/
NINE
RE/
WELL

DOLLHOUSE
Paint on wood
2007 /// Personal

Graphic Design

Illustration

  Dollhouse

  Computer Arts Magazine

  Tan The Man

  Helsinki in Berlin

  Tunto

  Scaniinavia Magazine

  Itella

  marimekko

  Acacom

  Altarpiece

  Finlandia Vodka

  Atria

  Metsa Tissue

  Sanoma Magazine

Summary
Creating a
Good Portfolio

1.

A good portfolio is one that showcases your work at its best and demonstrates that you understand what the commissioner who is looking at it requires.

2.

Taking stock of your creative strengths and weaknesses is as important as knowing the kind of work your target is looking for. Learn to be objective: only show samples in which you have confidence, and make sure they are all up to your highest standards. Leave out any that are self-indulgent.

3.

Creative employers take the contents of a portfolio at face value. If necessary, when putting one together add new samples that are relevant to a specific company's specialization and that demonstrate your versatility in their field. Illustrators should put images in an existing design or layout.

4.

Give published work pride of place in your portfolio, showing it sooner rather than later in your running order. And include one or two sketchbooks in case a commissioner is interested in seeing them at the end of the presentation.

5.

It may be necessary to put together more than one portfolio, or divide a single one into sections that show different disciplines and styles. In particular, multi-skilled practitioners may choose to have different portfolios that show skills that are specific to a variety of jobs.

Choosing the Right Portfolio

5

The way you decide to showcase your work will largely be determined by practicality and personal taste. Its scale, nature and application can all have a bearing on your choice, as may your budget and geographical location. For instance, sending an A3 print portfolio halfway across the world by courier is, for instance, costly and slow compared to emailing a client a PDF or a link to your website. Also, it goes without saying your samples should be immaculate and artfully displayed, but functionality is equally important. Whether you opt for a print or digital approach, or even, as is becoming increasingly common, a combination of the two, your portfolio should be logical and straightforward to negotiate, communicating your strengths as a practitioner clearly and concisely. Above all, it should engage the viewer's attention at the outset and hold it for the duration of the presentation.

Opposite: A custom-made portfolio with protective carrying case to fit, for a personalized presentation of work (see page 107).

The Digital Portfolio

Some types of work – notably motion graphics, interactive and web design – can't be shown to their full advantage in a print portfolio. Moreover, some commissioners and employers actively dislike print folders as they find viewing them a hassle. Even those who are print-oriented sometimes prefer to see a practitioner's work on a website or PDF before, or instead of, meeting them. Sites can be bookmarked, work can be viewed at leisure without any accompanying hard sell, and images are easily downloaded, shared with colleagues or forwarded to clients regardless of where in the world they are based.

'A website link can be entered easily into our employment database. CDs get lost in closets, paper gets swallowed by paper.'
Judy Wellfare, Creative Director, Plus et Plus

When it comes to face-to-face digital presentation, both laptops and tablet devices have many benefits. While a tablet weighs less than even one of the new generation of wafer-thin laptops, both weigh less than the average A3 print portfolio and take up significantly less desk space. One of the primary advantages of digital presentation is that work can be shown in a variety of ways: you can talk a potential employer through your personal website, blog, online portfolio, flickr page or similar; if your interests are primarily web-based you can demonstrate sites you've designed. There is also the option of using a slideshow or movie format, or simply presenting a selection of stills and/or moving images, any number of which can be taken to a meeting. For a relatively small outlay, you can buy an app that will allow you to present images and video, using a simple interface, on your tablet. In practice, any amount of portfolios can be taken to a meeting on a digital device, which can be useful for those with multiple skills, diverse target audiences or several illustrative styles. Both types of device permit work to be viewed on a larger screen using a projector or wireless streaming device.

Back when I was commissioned to write the first edition of this book, the iPad and its many imitators had yet to make their debut. In my opinion, the tablet has one advantage over the laptop. At the time of writing, the tablet lacks some of the software options and fancier functions of the laptop, but this is probably the reason why I find it preferable: laptop presentations can tend to go on too long and, when time is at a premium, that can come across as unprofessional. A tablet presentation has all the swiftness and ease of a print one and the gizmo itself can be passed around a meeting table as easily as a traditional portfolio. The interactive function of the tablet screen enables viewers to instantly resize and view details of images in ways that a laptop can't, and it's a simple intuitive process. So even though the screen is smaller, the tablet is in many ways more versatile, and resolution is becoming sharper all the time. On the downside, a digital device can't be left behind with a client like a print portfolio can, and clients who like to handle print samples will still be disappointed. There is also considerable scope for things to go wrong with a laptop presentation if you're not organized.

'Because we receive lots of communication from prospective interested parties, we can't meet all in person so a first level showing is best sent digitally. Then if we like it, we can meet in person.'
Anne Brassier, PR and New Business, Airside

What can go wrong?

I've suffered presentations shown on borrowed laptops with which the users were plainly unfamiliar; one was given on a laptop with its screen hanging off (the computer had been dropped the night before the presentation). And I've heard the words 'But it must be here! I transferred the file last night!' more times than I care to recall. People have arrived with a CD or memory stick, blithely assuming they will be giving their presentation on my computer without asking beforehand; others have assumed I've got Wi-Fi, (which I haven't always had). I've seen slideshow presentations with images timed to be lingered over for far too long, and have had to wait ages to view massive files that turned out to be life-drawings. I've seen typography and images that failed to display in the manner their creators intended them to (reversed out, for instance); and endured presentations that can best be described as the digital equivalent of upending the loose, unsorted contents of an A1 student portfolio – desktops crowded with files and random images that take forever to wade through, many of which aren't even relevant. I've even been shown subpar photographic images of pieces of work pinned to a studio wall, which is bad enough in a print portfolio. There is no excuse for any of this, least of all from someone whose speciality purports to be visual communication.

'Digital has increasingly become more viable as client computer tools have improved. Clients seem to appreciate not having to deal with physical portfolios, and they like the immediacy of email, and the ease of forwarding to colleagues. PDFs are definitely the preferred format now.'

Lance Hidy, freelance designer

How to get it right on a laptop

Firstly, have an overall plan and a logical running order. Because digital presentation is more complex than print, offering more options and flexibility, more thought needs to be given before a meeting as to what you show, how you show it and in what order. You may not have to mess around with scalpels and spray mount, but your objective doesn't change. It is to put together a judiciously selected body of work that highlights your skills with a minimum of fuss in a relatively short space of time. Images should be of the highest quality and quick and easy to access; websites, where applicable must be simple to negotiate (see chapter six). And it goes without saying that if web design is your area your own site should impress potential employers – although you don't want a triumph of style over functionality.

Like sketchbooks in a print portfolio, any additional material you take to a presentation is an optional extra as far as your interviewer is concerned. Should they express an interest in seeing more work in a similar vein during the course of the meeting, it will stand you in good stead to be organized in this respect. Categorizing your files and labelling your images so that you know exactly what's in them is the best way to ensure a swift and seamless response. Clicking on a succession of mystery JPGs is less likely to inspire confidence.

Secondly, become wholly self-reliant. Fully charge your laptop and pre-empt possible disasters by bringing appropriate back-up – this means cables and a power adaptor in case the laptop battery fails; CDs and/or a memory stick in case any of files mysteriously disappear or the server for your website is down; and some printed samples may not go amiss. If you

have mobile broadband, bring this too. In short, leave as little as possible to chance – and never assume you can use your client or future employer's computer; they are doing you a favour by agreeing to meet you in the first place. Always aim to give the presentation on your own laptop or, failing that, one you know how to use efficiently.

How to get it right on a tablet

Much of the above applies to tablet presentations too, at least with regard to brevity of running order and having an overall plan. However, a tablet presentation poses its own set of problems. See over the page for advice on how to overcome them.

Remote presentations

When you are targeting clients based in a different geographical location to yours, PDFs, DVDs, CDs, QuickTime movies, JPGs and similar, can be a godsend. However, always check that whatever you're planning to send will be welcome. Once again, make sure designs or images are tailored to the needs of the client and don't bombard them with hundreds of samples. Similarly, avoid huge files that take for ever to download.

'I like to see the actual work but also like to have the digital for future reference. Work at 100 per cent in size shows all details. A photo or an image scaled down on screen will easily hide imperfections in the work.'

Kristina DiMatteo, Art Director, *Print*

Presenting your portfolio digitally

Images displayed on tablets such as the iPad can be incredibly beautiful and easily presented as a portfolio. However, preparation of your images is crucial for success. It is important at this stage to give sufficient thought to how images might be used in a real world setting. You will need to be comfortable using design software to prepare your work for presentation on a tablet and be able to take crystal clear high resolution photos of your 2D work in preparation for digital presentation.

Preparing your work for digital presentation

If you are a digital illustrator or designer and already familiar with working in Adobe Illustrator, Photoshop or InDesign it is relatively easy to start the final imaging process digitally. Start your new portfolio image in a vector program (Illustrator) or raster program (Photoshop, Corel Painter) at high resolution. The colour space should be RGB. This is the name of the colour model, which mixes the primary colours red, green and blue. Save your portfolio images in the program's native format and archive the images.

Portfolio-quality drawings, paintings and other traditionally prepared works are a bit more complex to deal with since they must be either photographed or scanned at high resolution. 2D images must be evenly illuminated. These images must be aligned squarely to the viewfinder in the camera. Always use a tripod to steady your camera. It will allow you to take multiple exposures without the need for realignment. Take great care with this step. It can be somewhat frustrating, but well worth the effort.

Portfolio images should be recorded on camera in RAW format. RAW is the term used to describe unprocessed images before they are printed or edited. This format yields the most digital information and serves as your digital negative. These images will have to be adjusted. The most important adjustments will be colour, contrast, brightness and sharpening. Unwanted perspective (keystoning) and curvature also need adjustments. These operations can be accomplished using camera RAW software for your camera and Photoshop, saved in TIFF format and archived in a familiar filing system.

In preparation for formatting portfolio images for use on a tablet you need to make copies of the original files. Never alter originals and make sure all images are backed up for safety. Images for presentation should be formatted to double the longest dimension of the screen size. This measurement

for the current iPad screen is 2048 pixels, for example. As new versions are introduced this number may change. You will need to change the file type of the copies to .JPG and 'Save for Web & Devices' at high quality.

Store copies for easy access. Images stored on your computer can be synced to the iPad through iTunes. Pictures can also be stored in the 'cloud' using services such as Apple's iCloud or Dropbox. Both services make your images available on all your devices for convenient importation into presentation apps.

Using apps for tablet presentations

Numerous apps are available enabling various ways to exhibit your portfolio on tablet devices. Each is unique regarding the look and feel of presentations you may wish to display. These apps are relatively inexpensive and some are even free. Examples of these include Keynote, Portfolio, Padfolio and Minimal Portfolio. There are many others as well.

Keynote, part of Apple iWorks, is a presentation program similar to Microsoft Powerpoint. You can produce stylish presentations then display them as timed, self-running slide shows or reveal single images at your own pace. Either method of play offers interesting transitional effects. Padfolio includes features that allow you to have multiple portfolios in one location, enabling you to show the most appropriate collection of images. You can also choose to present portfolios in a similar fashion to Keynote.

There are creative options in all apps that can be selected by an artist to modify the way he or she wishes to display work. Portfolio presentations on a tablet are great if you're showing your work to one or two individuals, but may be a bit small for group presentations. As previously mentioned, a hugely beneficial option is that the machine can be toggled to a projector or large-screen video for larger groups.

And, to add extra impact to a presentation, the artist who has prepared and practised can have an entire toolbox of artist's materials at hand. There are numerous economically priced apps that allow an artist to use trimmed down versions of drawing, paint and page layout programs they are already familiar with. If the artist feels so inclined he or she can do a digital painting or photo-manipulation right in the client's office as they watch. This can be an impressive sight, especially when done by someone who really knows the capabilities of the apps.

The Print Portfolio

Art directors/editors who predominantly work in and commission for print are, as a rule, happy to see a portfolio that speaks their language – though it is also acceptable to present storyboards for website design in a print portfolio. As presentations go, print is just about bombproof. The folder is quick to view, is easily passed around during a meeting, and work is readily accessible for photocopying or scanning; it is also invaluable for back-up or drop-off purposes. There are no fiddly, unreliable peripherals to carry around, and no batteries, Wi-Fi or connections are required, so you'll be immune to freak weather conditions, server problems and electricity cuts. Print also makes sound economic sense for cash-strapped novice practitioners, since even the most deluxe portfolios on the market tend to be cheaper than most tablets or laptops. There is a limit to the amount of work you can physically carry to a meeting; however, it is easy to email further samples to anyone who expresses a desire to see more.

'It's good to have something tactile to thumb through. Also easier to show clients in a meeting. Some clients have old crappy PCs that can't display such things as JPGs. Also, you don't have to worry about your computer failing in a meeting.'

Steve Rutterford, Art Director, Brooklyn Brothers

Size matters

There's a reason why A3 (16.9 × 12 inch) and A4 (8.5 × 12 inch) – rather than A1 (24 × 33.9 inch), A2 (16.9 × 24 inch), or even A0 (33.9 × 24 inch) – portfolios have become the industry norm. You can't rely on having access to a vast boardroom table on which to spread out your work. Most of the time practitioners present their portfolios in their target's actual workspace – more often than not a small space or studio. Desk and floor space will be at a serious premium and a portfolio of manageable size (one small and light enough for the interviewer to place it comfortably in their lap and flick through it), will be greatly appreciated. From your point of view, an A3 or A4 portfolio is cheaper to post, and easier to courier to locally based clients. The most common reason for persisting with a huge portfolio is lack of funds or not having larger pieces of work reduced.

Published designs

Given that it is preferable to show published work in context wherever possible, I favour A3 over A4, for all the latter's compact, lightweight charms. A design for a double-page spread or wraparound book jacket can be comfortably accommodated within a single page – whereas an A4 portfolio demands they either be sliced in two or reduced to half-size in order to display them. In the case of the former, clunky ring binding or a substantial gap between the separate halves can be off-putting, as they interrupt the visual flow and lessen the overall impact of the design. In addition, storyboards retain more detail, and sets – of packaging or book covers, for example – look more impressive when displayed at full size in groups larger than A4 permits; and poster designs retain more visual clout at A3. If a design features illustrations, and particularly if the printed images aren't all that big, the reduction to half-size can make them difficult to read or easy to overlook; the same goes for work that is quite delicate or densely detailed. You, however, may think differently; many practitioners find an A4 portfolio meets their needs more than adequately.

Original illustrations

Illustrators, especially those working at a large scale in non-digital media, may want clients to see their work in its original form, maintaining that subtleties of colour and texture are lost when it is printed. While some commissioners appreciate having the opportunity to see originals, it's important to remember that illustrations are primarily created to be reproduced. Clients are therefore more concerned with seeing how a work will look in a printed context than what it might look like on a gallery wall. (No printed job is ever a precise colour-match to the artwork, so there's little point agonizing about this. Instead, take comfort in the knowledge that some of printed pieces may look better than the originals.) If your artwork is flexible and you are determined to show originals larger than A3 or A4, roll a couple of illustrations up and put them in a lightweight tube with a handle or shoulder strap. Even if your artwork is small enough to be incorporated in an A3 or A4 portfolio, it is advisable to show good-quality digital print-outs rather than precious originals, in case of accidental damage or loss (as anyone else who has left a portfolio on a train will tell you; I got mine back but it was the longest ten days of my life).

What kind of portfolio?

The wide variety of portfolio types, formats and systems on the market ranges through soft-covered folders with fixed or removable plastic leaves to ring-bound, zip-up ones with hard cases, portfolio boxes for presenting loose samples, and luxury models that, for a price, can be tailored to individual needs. And there is nothing to stop anyone who feels so inclined creating or customizing their own portfolio. Finishes on off-the-shelf folders vary widely, and nowhere is it stipulated that covers must be regulation black imitation (or genuine) leather. I've seen them covered in blue denim, Day-Glo pink PVC and – on one memorable occasion – AstroTurf. If you want to stand out from the crowd, by all means go for it – just don't lose sight of the fact it's what's inside the portfolio that counts.

'It depends on the type of work (web work does not present well in a traditional print portfolio format).'

Doug Powell, Creative Director, Schwartz Powell Design

A bound portfolio has the obvious advantage that it keeps all your work together, so individual pieces are less likely to go astray during a drop-off; while employers and commissioners who find a bound format preferable do so because it is easy, simple and speedy to view. However, it is best to choose a design that allows you to add or remove leaves according to your requirements. That way you won't be restricted as to how many pieces you can include; nor (should your selection of work be less than extensive) will you be left with a lot of empty leaves. This can happen if a practitioner opts for the cheapest kind of folder, where the leaves are an integral part of the design – though similar problems can occur at the pricier end of the market. One illustrator I know had to have all the leaves replaced by the company that manufactured her custom-made portfolio every time she wanted to add a new sample or change the running order. What's more, she had to pay (albeit a nominal fee) for the privilege. Flexibility is another factor to take into consideration when considering your options.

Some commissioners of design are less keen on a bound format, preferring to handle individual samples of work. While it's great to be able to give them the option – graphic design is, after all, intended to be touched, used, read and explored – this isn't always practicable. If you are presenting college projects or personal work, having it handled shouldn't pose too much of a problem providing you can produce an identical sample when the old one starts to look a little worn (say, after the twenty-fifth art director has played with it). However, where published work is concerned, it isn't always possible to rely on having more than one sample, and sometimes even this is difficult to obtain. In this instance, get high-resolution images made of the work in question. These can be printed out and displayed conventionally in a print portfolio or uploaded to a digital one, and you have the option of taking the originals to clients who may want to handle them.

Leaves and laminates

Regardless of the format you decide on your work should always be protected, especially if you're showing originals or samples that are expensive, time consuming or impossible to replace. Leaves in various sizes are readily available for portfolio boxes and ring-bound portfolios; and practitioners who want to show loose samples can have them individually laminated. Colours may look slightly muted beneath a layer of shiny plastic, but this is preferable to having someone spill their coffee all over your work or, worse still, burn a hole in it.

'They should be mounted in sleeves. It illustrates attention to detail and a better presentation to me. The mounted pages can, of course, be loose if in a box portfolio but a jumble of work in a case doesn't look professional or organized.'

Richard Ogle, Art Director, Random House

'Print presentations are great. My old print portfolio is very trustworthy though rarely updated. A lot of people present portfolios online. I also like to show sketchbooks and process.'

Josh Keay, freelance designer

Opposite: For those who lean towards something more luxurious, custom-made portfolios are available at a price. These embossed, leather-bound folders were made by Brodies, a specialist London-based company who manufacture portfolios to individual specifications.

Below: Some practitioners, like illustrator Lydia Fee, prefer to design their own portfolio or customize an existing design in order to stand out from the crowd.

How to display your work

If your work is dark and dense with a gothic vibe, mounting images on black is not a good idea. Ditto mounting pale, delicate and ethereal work on white. Unless it is to your advantage, forget whatever you were told at college: work doesn't have to be mounted on black or white – or even buff or grey. In fact, some pieces needn't necessarily be mounted. Some illustrators print out images with a full bleed and this is also acceptable. Where applicable, an illustration should be mounted on whatever colour background makes it shine – and if, in your opinion, this happens to be brown Harris tweed or lavender tissue paper, so be it. Obviously, though, the mount should always flatter rather than dominate an image.

'(A print portfolio) is much quicker to look through, and can be passed around. Also, we design for print, not the web.'
Eleanor Crow, Art Director, The Folio Society

Try to avoid placing mounts within mounts within mounts; you're assembling a portfolio for industry not submitting your work to the Venice Biennale - and, above all, whether you are a designer or an illustrator, avoid bulky mounting board. Not only will your folder weigh a ton, but in many ring-bound portfolios the leaves are suspended from a central spine to which the handle is attached. Heavy mounting board will put extra strain on the leaves and soon split the eyelets. Replacing portfolio leaves on a regular basis is costly, and there's only so much you can do with a scalpel and adhesive tape before replacement becomes your only option. Opt for a mount made from good-quality paper or lightweight card instead of board, with any descriptive text, should it be necessary, discreetly printed on it; sticky labels and handwritten Post-Its look amateurish.

Another way to make a portfolio twice as heavy as it needs to be is to show only one sample per spread, leaving the facing page blank. In the world around us graphics and illustration compete with rival images. Think how often you walk past a wall displaying dozens of posters and flyers, or flick through a magazine where some of the advertisements are scarcely distinguishable from the editorial. Scores of newly released books, CDs, DVDs, computer games and movies constantly compete for our visual attention. Trust me, two pieces of work can coexist on the same spread without losing visual impact or cancelling

each other out. If they can't, the chances are one of them wasn't all that good to begin with.

Lastly, both designers and illustrators may need to decide how to display both portrait- and landscape-format samples in a portfolio. While the ideal is to feature a 'matching pair' on every spread, this is not always possible. So try to minimize the amount of folder-twirling your interviewer will have to do by deciding in which direction both formats will face, and abiding by that decision throughout your portfolio.

'I've never been bowled over by a portfolio. Only its contents.'
Steve Rutterford, Art Director, Brooklyn Brothers

Photographs of samples

If you want your portfolio to feature work that needs to be photographed – window displays, exhibition designs, murals, or unwieldy or three-dimensional artworks – get it photographed by someone who knows what they're doing or invest in a decent camera and tripod and do it yourself. Even today I'm routinely shown cheap, out-of-focus snapshots of illustrators' work leaning against a garden fence on an overcast day – and there's simply no excuse for this kind of unprofessionalism. The same advice applies to work so delicate that it won't survive too much handling by overzealous commissioners.

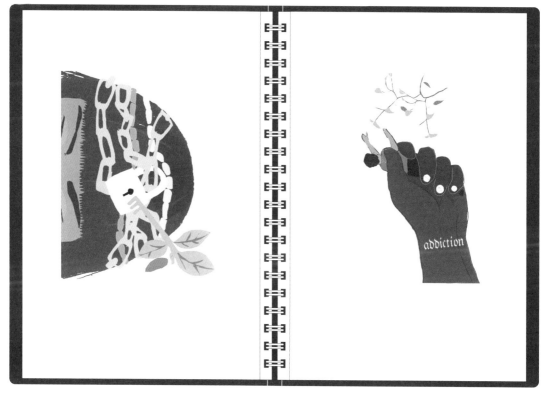

Face and fortune

As Western populations grow older, the pressure to look young grows stronger. As she nears her 50th birthday, **Daphne Merkin** must decide whether to face up to her age, or succumb to the surgeon's knife. Illustrations by **Stuart Briers**

> If you haven't gone under the surgeon's knife by 50, it seems, yours is the face nature meant you to have – the face, that is, of an incipient hag

Housing Illustration

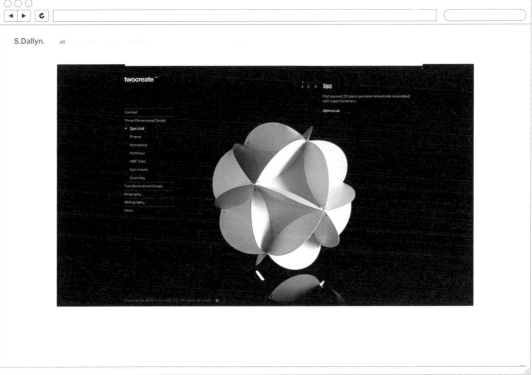

Summary
Choosing the
Right Portfolio

1.

A portfolio should be logical and straightforward to negotiate, with samples immaculately and clearly displayed. It must engage the viewer's attention from the start and hold it throughout the presentation.

2.

A print portfolio can be viewed quickly and easily, and samples can be scanned or photocopied. A3 and A4 folders are the norm, although A3 is often preferable to A4 if you are showing published work in context.

3.

Print portfolios are available in a variety of types, formats and systems. A bound one keeps all the samples together so that they are less likely to go astray, while a portfolio box allows the interviewer to handle the work.

4.

Regardless of the type of portfolio its contents must be protected, either in leaves or, if the samples are loose, by laminating the individual pieces of work. And avoid heavy mounting board; instead use good-quality paper or lightweight cardboard.

5.

Work such as motion graphics and web design is best shown on a digital portfolio, while some creative employers positively prefer to see print samples on a website or as PDFs as they can be easily shown to colleagues or sent to clients.

6.

Use a laptop for face-to-face presentations. It is lightweight, takes up little space on a desk and allows you to show your work in a variety of ways.

Opposite: Art director/designer Sam Dallyn's flash-based online portfolio showcases his work cleanly. Shown here are a website designed for luxurious hotel group Le Meridien (top) and another for cross-disciplinary design studio Two Create (bottom).

Making Yourself Known in the Marketplace

6

It is important to meet personally with creative employers and commissioners wherever and whenever you can. Since job advertisements for junior designers with less than a year or two's experience are rare, and ones for illustrators virtually non-existent (advertisements placed by agents who want to swell their books don't count and are no guarantee of work), it will be up to you to be proactive and make yourself known in the creative marketplace by whatever means possible. Getting on well with a potential employer, discovering you're on the same creative wavelength or share similar interests can give you a real advantage if and when a vacancy or suitable commission does come up.

Opposite: A D&AD Portfolio Surgery, where industry creatives share their expertise with students and new designers, giving advice on portfolio formats, structuring and editing.

Networking Pays Off

One advantage of the face-to-face interview is that even though your contact may not have a vacancy or commission that is suitable for you, they may know someone who has – and, when it comes to making industry connections, personal recommendation has the distinct advantage over cold-calling. So, whenever a client or commissioner gives you positive feedback, ask if they know of anyone else who might like your work. If an art director/editor knows you've been recommended by a fellow practitioner familiar with their taste and requirements, there's a strong likelihood they'll agree to meet you, and the more contacts you make the more recommendations you're likely to receive. And don't worry too much if the person you show your portfolio to isn't in a senior position. Firstly, many creatives progress quickly in their chosen fields; and secondly, in some areas junior members of design departments work on exciting projects as their ideas are considered the freshest. Meeting a future art director/editor could give you precisely the break you need.

'I need to get great samples or a recommendation from someone I know before I will meet. With either of those, I'm happy to meet.'

Steve Scott, Art Director, Scholastic

In some respects the creative industry has changed surprisingly little in the decades since I left art college. However, as a fledgling designer I was without the benefit of the web and had few resources at my disposal, so had little recourse but to blindly blanket-bomb my way through the *Creative Handbook* – 'blanket-bomb' because, unless a design group was well known or had taken out an advertisement in addition to paying for a listing, there was no means of knowing the kind of work it produced or in which areas it might specialize. It was a slow, demoralizing process, which is why I don't recommend it. I systematically worked my way through the listings, firing off 15–20 letters every other week, mostly to companies I knew nothing about. A third of them, at most, got back to me, and of these two or three agreed to look at my portfolio.

Fortunately, designers today have a lot more information than I had when I was selecting appropriate targets, but you could do worse than follow my lead in one respect. I told the recipients of my letters that I realized they didn't have any jobs going, but said I was sure I would benefit hugely from their professional opinion regardless, and asked if they'd be so generous as to lend me a few minutes of their precious time. I freely confess I was lying. While professional feedback is not to be disregarded, the real reason I dragged myself back and forth to those often fruitless interviews was the vague hope that, eventually, someone would not only like my portfolio, but would also reveal they had a vacancy for a junior designer which hadn't yet been publicized – and it turned out that quite a few of them had. I was shortlisted a couple of times, then landed my first job, which was an invaluable, month-long, cash-in-hand no-questions-asked internship. I was subsequently offered another job and also a paid three-month internship with a top London branding consultancy – both during the week I finally landed a full-time job elsewhere through the college grapevine. Networking can be hard graft but, eventually, it pays off.

Since illustrators rarely have the option of securing full-time employment, networking is for them an ongoing process, so make the most of every opportunity that comes your way. Occasionally, a promotional piece you send to a client will either be exactly what they're looking for (in which case they might ask you if it has already been used and, if it hasn't, pay you for it), or bears enough resemblance to what they want for them to commission you to do a similar illustration without the benefit of an interview. Many illustrators, having been commissioned in this way, sometimes multiple times, never bother to suggest a meeting. Obviously setting one up isn't always practicable, but if a client is within a reasonable distance, don't hesitate. Commissioners pigeonhole illustrators; a personal meeting will give you the opportunity to broaden their horizons when it comes to how else they might use you. They may spot something in your portfolio and reappraise your skills as result.

It's a frustrating fact of life that sometimes potential employers can't always spare the time to meet with new talent. However there will always be opportunities to connect in an informal setting. Subscribing to industry Twitter feeds can keep you up to date on all kinds of events such as private views, lectures, conferences, book launches, competitions, award ceremonies and exhibitions; as will linking to design-related blog posts and discussions. You may even get the heads-up about a job opportunity. Most companies – the publishers of this book, for instance – have a Facebook page for keeping followers up-to-date with their activities. Other social networking sites, such as Linked In, Google+, Ning, etc., can also be used to research or connect with industry; professional interest groups abound.

Pitching for a Presentation

An unsolicited telephone call works for some practitioners, but you'll need nerves of steel unless you sold advertising space or worked in a call centre in a previous life. The higher up the ladder and the more in demand your target is, the harder it will be to get past their personal assistant. The following advice may be unorthodox but it has, nonetheless, served me well. When asked who you are and what your business is, instead of saying, 'I'm an unknown designer/illustrator who's desperate to show your boss my work' simply give just your first name as casually as you can. There is a good chance the PA will assume you're a friend, relative or lover, and put you straight through. Failing this, attend industry events (award ceremonies, private views, or professional seminars), with the express purpose of meeting your more elusive targets.

'A CV and its design are critical, as are no typos in the CV or cover letter. I also ask for three samples of things candidates are inspired by. On one occasion I have hired someone on the spot because of what she brought.'

Josh Silverman, President/Founder/Minister of Perspective, Schwadesign, Inc.

Sending unsolicited emails often has a disappointing outcome, though you may be asked to submit your details via email when responding to a specific job advertisement. If you are making a speculative approach to a potential employer I would always advise sending a letter. This should be grammatically perfect, without a single typo or spelling error, regardless of whether you are writing in your mother tongue or not – if necessary, ask someone who speaks your target's language to check the letter before you send it – and it should be addressed to a named contact. A letter riddled with lower case 'i's or text-speak will be thrown away in an instant, as will one that starts 'Dear Sir/Madam' or 'To Whom It May Concern' (particularly if the company is named after the individual you're targeting and the name makes their sex obvious).

Your letter should be polite, focused and succinct, and should never exceed one side of an A4 (8.5 × 12 inch) sheet. As well as introducing you as a practitioner, it should make clear you are aware of the kind of work your target does, and how your skills might be relevant, if not immediately obvious. For example, if you are an aspiring book-jacket designer you

might, when approaching a suitable publisher, say something along the lines of: 'I was interested in your striking repackaging of so-and-so's backlist for Penguin. As you can see from the attached samples, which formed part of my final major project prior to graduation, literary fiction is one of my main interests as a designer.'

Meanwhile, an illustrator who specializes in food, gardening and travel could write: 'I very much enjoyed your inventive redesign of X's range of herbal teas and enclose a copy of a piece on Chinese herbal medicine that I illustrated for the November edition of *Good Housekeeping*.'

Your choice of paper, the typeface you use and the way in which you lay out your letter should reflect your creative persona and professionalism, as should your letterhead if you have one. If you don't, I suggest you rethink the situation. At this stage you need to do everything in your power to whet the appetite of potential employers or clients. A memorable, well-designed letterhead can be as effective in engaging their attention as more complex projects in your portfolio; it could be the reason they choose to look at your portfolio.

For designers, whether they are making a speculative pitch or applying for an advertised position, it's customary to include a curriculum vitae (CV) that expands on any skills and achievements touched on in their introductory letter. Anything that exceeds two sides of an A4 sheet is too long and reverse chronological order tends to be the accepted norm. Your CV signposts your abilities and therefore needs to be as visually representative of the way you think and communicate as the rest of your portfolio. While some employers put more faith in the contents of a newcomer's CV than others, most expect to see solid evidence of typographic skills and personal flair.

By contrast, a CV is as much use to an illustrator as the proverbial chocolate teapot. If you've worked for notable or impressive clients include the information in your covering letter and concentrate on choosing some strong, representative samples for your portfolio.

'I'm most interested in the CV. Not only for what it says, but what it doesn't say and how the information is presented.'

Robert Linsky, Senior Vice President of Design, Art Plus Technology

HELLO PROFERO, MY NAME IS DARREN CUSTANCE, AND QUITE SIMPLY I WANT TO WORK FOR YOU.

ABOUT

I am a graphic designer who has been interested in your work at Profero for a while now. I was especially intrigued by your work for ASOS marketplace and how you created "the people's runway".

Hopefully my attached portfolio will demonstrate my own creative thinking and strong work ethic and I look forward to hearing from you soon.

I am an enthusiastic designer with a passion to push the boundaries of visual communication.

With great self-belief and a competitive drive, I enjoy experimenting and creating new, innovative solutions to any visual problem. Proactive and motivated, I thrive in pressurised environments whilst still possessing strong abilities to perform effectively.

I am very interested in the social context of design, as we possess the tools to influence societies and cultures.

CONTACT

Darren Custance
Design and Art Direction

Phone
+44 (0) 7402850598

Website
cargocollective.com/darrencustance

Email
darrencustance@hotmail.com

AGENCIES

The Partners: London
One Month Placement
June 2011

Engine Creative: Northampton
Two Week Placement
April 2011

Milton Bayer: Northampton
One Year Placement
September 2010 - June 2011

EDUCATION

1st Class Degree Classification
BA (Hons) Graphic Communication
The University of Northampton
2008 - 2011

Stocks Taylor Benson Star of the Show
BA (Hons) Graphic Communication
The University of Northampton
2011

TAGS

Software
Adobe CS5 Photoshop, Illustrator, InDesign, After effects, Final cut pro

Skills
Conceptualising, problem solving, digital, interactive design, multichannel design, art direction, style guidelines, UX design, colour theory, iconography, advertising, film, story boarding, hand rendered typography, screen printing, print design, packaging design, product design, point of sale design, outdoor design, in-store design, branding, brand guidelines, logo design, illustration, blogging.

DC

'For me the CV is the most important piece of promotional material. The number of dreadful CVs I see is staggering. If they can't design a CV they probably can't design.'

Colin McHenry, Group Art Director, Centaur Media

Below: The quirky, tactile CV of Camberwell MA student Alix Jeambrun, a multi-skilled practitioner who frequently combines collage and stitch in her illustration work.

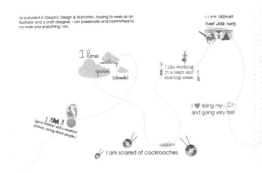
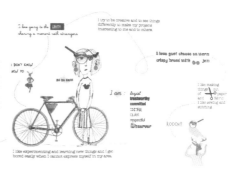

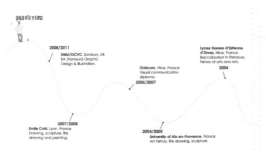
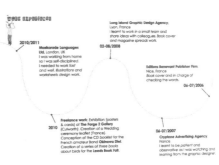

Below: Rob Ryan, with his distinctive cut-paper and silkscreen print work, is also a self-marketing whizz. His London store, Ryantown, sells his work complete with promotional material as part of the shopping experience. Ryan's distinctive style lends a magical air to a central London branch of Coutts Bank. His Christmas window was created to raise money for the charity, Kids Company.

'I don't think there needs to be a huge promotional gimmick. It is much more important to focus on a strong, consistent portfolio.'

Jennifer Pastore, Associate Photo Editor, *The New York Times Style Magazine*

Promotional Material

Promotional samples can function as an introduction to your work before you see a creative employer or as a reminder of it after a meeting has taken place. They vary tremendously, and range from simple computer print-outs to professionally printed postcards and broadsheets, run-ons from advertisements in sourcebooks or samples included in annuals, self-packaged DVDs of motion graphics or animation, and self-published books – as well as novelty items such as mugs, badges, stickers and mouse mats. It is best to offer novelties as leave-behinds after a meeting, rather than using them as a means of introduction; creative opinion is vastly divided over them and some professionals find attention-getting devices seriously annoying.

Try to avoid overkill. A general, all-purpose piece of promotional material, plus one or two carefully selected samples of your best work, beautifully printed out on good-quality paper, is more likely to persuade your target to meet you than sending them the entire contents of your portfolio. They are likely to be busy, and too many examples of your work will give them the perfect excuse to avoid seeing you: 'Well, we've got a pretty good idea of your range here, so we'll just keep it on file in case something comes up in the future.' Your meeting is strangled at birth and so is any spur-of-the-moment job opportunity or further recommendations.

It goes without saying that all promotional samples should have your name and contact details on them, whether the format is digital or print. I strongly advise against the use of CDs unless this is specifically requested, as many commissioners dislike them. The simplicity and immediacy of the printed image cannot be underestimated.

Of course, these days there's a good deal more to self promotion than printed material and novelty leave-behinds. You can also whet the appetite of future employers – and retain their interest – by using the same tools you'd use to find out what they're up to. Those who work with moving images can share their work with industry on youtube or vimeo; collectives can tweet about their latest collaborations. My best friend, a children's book illustrator, has boosted her income considerably since creating a Facebook account, through which she now receives regular private commissions. Like many creative practitioners she uploads recent work, shares that of other creative practitioners, and provides links to her own blog and her agent's. She also promotes the limited edition zines, stickers and badges she sells in her Folksy store. Others may choose to use resources like Tumblr, Pinterest or Deviant Art to attract the attention of potential clients.

Digital Media

I won't lie; not every personal project has the potential to make its creator heaps of money. As always, luck has a part to play. However, because the internet gives practitioners the potential to share some of their quirkier obsessions with millions worldwide, it's no surprise that many cult blogs and curated collections have made the leap into print in recent years. After all, editors have to have something to alleviate the tedium of working their way through the slush pile, and these days they're just as likely to uncover a potential gem online. The following pages present some inspirational examples.

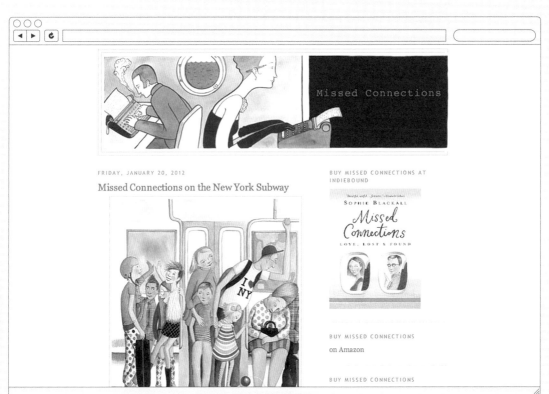

Case study
Missed Connections:
Sophie Blackall's blog

Opposite: (Top) Sophie still updates the original Missed Connections blog. This screen capture showcases the mural she did for Arts In Transit.
(Bottom left) The Missed Connections book, and (right) one of the earliest illustrations Sophie did for the blog. The man in the bear suit also features in the Arts In Transit frieze, sadly without his girlfriend and in possession of both parts of the costume.

Until word spread about Sophie Blackall's charming and idiosyncratic blog, Missed Connections, she was primarily known as a children's book illustrator. An Australian who relocated to Brooklyn 14 years ago with her family, Sophie discovered the Craig's List star-crossed lonely hearts section as a result of a chance meeting on a train. Whereas some may have fallen for the handsome stranger who clued her in, Sophie instead fell in love with the concept. The surreal content of some of the ads inspired the blog – Sophie's first – in March 2009. Career wise, it has since proved to be something of a game changer.

Initially the blog was a secret, an escape from Sophie's children's work and an experiment in self discipline. However, she quickly realized that her original intention to post one illustration a day – each taking no longer than an hour – was unworkable and eventually settled on one a week. Such is the power of the re-blog if something resonates with enough kindred spirits, that by this time a small community of enthusiastic commentators had begun to form around Missed Connections. The realization that Sophie now had an audience strengthened her resolve to keep up the momentum. Six months after the project's inception *The New York Times* ran a feature on it, followed swiftly by various other publications based further afield. Sophie, who was beginning to wonder whether there might be a book in it, was subsequently approached by no less than a dozen US book publishers, eventually opting to go with Workman. The eventual result, which features 46 images from the blog and 10 new ones, was published in 2011, exposing Sophie to a considerably wider, international client base.

Although Sophie continues to illustrate children's books she now receives commissions she wouldn't previously have been in the running for. One such was a poster design for New York's Metropolitan Transport Authority – an honour bestowed upon only two artists per year. The resulting frieze, depicting a typically mismatched and colourful bunch of travellers, was featured in the carriages of half the trains in the city. However, although the project had in effect come full circle, the ripples it created continued to impact on Sophie's career. As the blog began to flourish, Sophie had joined the Etsy community, selling Missed Connections prints in her virtual store. When she got the Arts For Transit commission, Etsy made a short film about Sophie's work for their blog and further commissions followed. Currently she is about to start work on a project for the international public health charity, The Measles and Rubella Initiative; drawing on location at immunization clinics in central Africa in order to produce a book, an animation, or both to raise awareness and funding for the project.

Sophie's journey has been, in her own words, 'a dream ride' in terms of personal fulfilment, and she strongly advises new illustrators to start a blog of their own, regardless of theme. Over the past few years she has continued to increase her internet presence with a professional website and blog, a Facebook page, and her latest personal project, Drawn From My Father's Adventures.

I AM → PLEASED TO INFORM YOU BY THIS MEDIUM

GENUINE EURO EMAIL LOTTERY WINNER

Case study
Secret Weapon: 30 SPAM Postcards
Linzie Hunter

Opposite and below: A selection of images from the Secret Weapon postcard book, demonstrating Linzie's distinctive approach to colour and hand lettering.

These days London-based Scot Linzie Hunter is known for her distinctive hand lettering, but it wasn't always this way; she has Flickr and the unwanted contents of her inbox to thank for transforming her illustration career. Finding some of the more baroque examples of spam she received highly amusing, Linzie spent a weekend producing an experimental series of hand-lettered responses to their outlandish claims. Since she already archived her work on Flickr, she uploaded these swiftly executed pieces as a set, where they still remain to this day.

As is the way of the internet, a fellow artist saw Linzie's 'spam one-liners' and sent a link to the illustration-centric blog, Drawn. Subsequent re-blogging led to coverage on geekblogs Boing Boing and Wired. However it wasn't until *The New York Times* journalist, Rob Walker, decided to give it a write-up in his eco-themed Consumed column, that Linzie's fortunes seriously began to change. Bizarrely, none of her images even appeared in the piece, which promoted the project as a sterling example of recycling. Nonetheless Linzie's website recorded an epic number of hits and she was approached by several US publishers, including Chronicle, who eventually published *Secret Weapon* in 2009. She was also approached by New York gallery owner Jen Bekman with a view to turning some of the pieces into limited edition prints for her online venture 20 X 200. This has proved to be a successful and lucrative partnership.

Currently Linzie receives around 70% of her work from the US, where the hand lettered book jacket commissions that came her way in the wake of *Secret Weapon* have made her immensely popular and taken her work in directions she'd never anticipated. Aware that commissioners frequently comb the internet for inspiration, Linzie has cultivated a sizeable online presence. In addition to her Flickr archive she has a personal website, Facebook, Linked-In and Twitter accounts and an online portfolio on Behance, which has resulted in prestigious advertising campaigns for clients such as Nike, MTV and Gillette. Linzie has also garnered commissions through her involvement in the invitation-only blogging site Drawger and its portfolio-hosting spin-off site, Illoz.

Below: For their 2008 Christmas promotion,
independent design consultancy
MARC&ANNA chose something eminently
practical – a tea towel to mop up the
inevitable mess over the festive season.

'One-off promotional things have got to be absolutely brilliant.'

Neil Dawson, Global Creative Director, Philips, DDB

Below: UK outfit Because Studio produced this limited print run of 50 handmade self-promotional books, featuring a selection of projects undertaken over a six-month period.

'I never really look at the CV, just the work. The more inventive the promotional material the better.'

Andy Altman, Partner/Creative Director, Why Not Associates

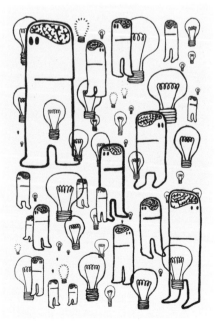

Opposite: Girls Who Draw are a collective of multidisciplinary freelancers engaged in promoting their skills to a wider audience. Their self-promotional work includes (top row) the *Love to Print* postcard box, designed by Yee Ting Kuit, and card design by Gemma Correll, and (bottom row) group book, *Misfits*, including postcard design by Bogus Baby.

Below: Illustrator Jay Taylor's chosen method of self-promotion is the mini-book (top row). So effective was his first edition, *Illustration Illustrated*, that he has since produced a follow-up, *Throw-Away Art*. Barnaby Richards (bottom row) has produced three books in this self-published series. With a print run of 1,000 each they were sold internationally, even retailing in Paul Smith's store, New York.

Presentation Pointers

Most creative employers dress like slightly upmarket versions of their student selves: jeans, T-shirts, trainers, retro-geek glasses and a fair amount of black. In other words, unless your target has a meeting scheduled with a corporate client or their bank manager, they're unlikely to be dressed like them when they interview you. This is particularly pertinent to designers and illustrators who are making speculative presentations. These tend to be informal, so dress for them in a way that makes you feel confident, smart (according to your definition of the word) and physically comfortable. On the other hand, if you are meeting a non-creative client as a freelance designer or an illustrator, you may wish to dress more formally depending on the field in which they work. For instance, people in the corporate or financial sector tend to be happier in the company of suits rather than tattoos and piercings.

'I have made strong referrals on behalf of entry-level designers who have impressed me with their composure, professionalism, candor…and, yes, their strong portfolio.'

Doug Powell, Creative Director, Schwartz Powell Design

Whatever you choose to wear, there are rules that must be followed:

Be punctual. If you are seriously early for an appointment, kill some time in a café; if you are late, don't be surprised if your reception is less than cordial. Arriving on time indicates you are reliable and this is of paramount importance to employers, commissioners and clients.

Make and maintain friendly eye contact with your interviewer/s. For some years I taught on a creative-career management course where, to learn how to sell themselves to clients, students from various disciplines were encouraged to interview each other as role play. Many of them avoided all eye contact; instead they stared into space or at the floor while they spoke about their work and college life. They couldn't have communicated less.

Show you've done your homework. Make sure you know about the company or individual you are meeting.

Be prepared

Some of the items in this list may seem obvious, but many practitioners believe that all they need to bring to a presentation is their portfolio, and are ill-prepared for potential problems or any requests an interviewer may make.

The address and telephone number of your destination. And a street map or Google map won't go amiss. It's not worth taking the risk of arriving late at a meeting because you've lost your way. Why leave being punctual to chance if chance makes you look unprofessional?

Your mobile phone (in case of delay or emergency).

Extra copies of your CV, if applicable; business cards and promotional material. You may be introduced to more contacts than you expected.

Your diary and a notebook and working pen. You may want to take notes. And what if you are asked to take a brief at a meeting or schedule a second interview?

Major back-up if you are giving a digital presentation (see chapter five).

'Don't fill your time at an interview by talking. Keep quiet unless answering a question. You don't want to create an opportunity to say the wrong thing. Sometimes the silence at an interview is a test.'

Kristina DiMatteo, Art Director, *Print*

Presenting Your Portfolio

Whether you are a designer or an illustrator, you need to think objectively about your creative strengths and interests, and be prepared to talk about them.

Because part of a designer's remit is making presentations to (and, eventually, on behalf of), the company they work for, the ability to speak intelligently and succinctly about your work will be as much under scrutiny as the work itself. Daunting as this may seem, what it really means is being able to define the problems posed by each project, and explaining how you solved them and why you opted for the solutions you did. Along with familiarizing yourself with the work of a potential employer, marshalling these facts before a presentation is a sure way to boost your confidence. (Freelance designers should take note that non-creative clients are primarily interested in what they did, rather than how they arrived at the solution.)

'Great work, well edited in a manageable book, plus a personable, professional person who can talk intelligently about their work.'

Steve Scott, Art Director, Scholastic

Creative employers aren't looking for cocksure hard sell; by and large, they want logical thinking, creative understanding and talent – plus a personality they feel they can work with. They're also looking for honesty, which means you can admit to your weaknesses. No one appreciates someone who exaggerates their skills, and if you do this you're sure to be found out – like the interviewee who tried to pass himself off as a graduate of the Royal College of Art in London to two of its alumni, who had been students at the college during the period he claimed to have been there.

'It is a very small industry, everyone knows everyone, and so while ambition is a good attribute, modesty and honesty will get you much further than bullshitting. It is also really important to give accurate credit to the teams and companies that you have worked or collaborated with.'

Judy Wellfare, Creative Director, Plus et Plus

When it comes to how much talking you do, take your cue from the interviewer. While many creative employers like to be talked through every project in a portfolio, and ask a lot of questions along the way, some prefer to concentrate on the work without a running commentary. The first time I encountered one of the latter – a publishing art director – I thought him rude and clearly disinterested in what I was showing him. I couldn't have been more mistaken. Despite refusing to laugh at any of my finely honed anecdotes, or being especially responsive to anything I told him about the artists, he was logging their skills for future reference. About a week after the presentation, which I'd written off as a disaster, he called up with two book jackets that were absolutely perfect for two illustrators whose work he'd seen. An unwillingness to chat can simply indicate intense concentration. My advice to all practitioners is to offer to tell a contact a little about each sample, invite them to ask you for more information if needed, and then take it from there.

'A lot of it, over and above talent, is down to personality. If someone is talented but annoying, we won't employ them. Conversely, if someone is getting there with room for improvement, but open and willing, we won't rule them out.'

Anne Brassier, PR and New Business, Airside

Below: A fast-loading, easily negotiable
and well-designed personal website is
a must. Pictured here are the websites
of (from top) multidisciplinary design
company Remote Location, designer/
typographer/photographer Caroline
Fabes, and children's book illustrator,
Polly Dunbar.

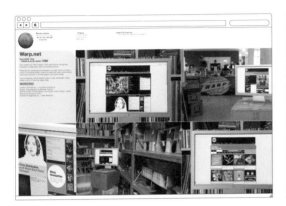

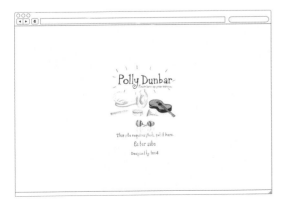

Post-presentation Reminders

In addition to self-promotional leave-behinds and the judicious use of social networking sites there are many other ways to remind hard-won contacts of your existence. Start by sending them a thank-you note in whatever format you like – they're more likely to read an email once they've met you, particularly if they liked your work. This provides you with a legitimate excuse to send a few more samples of your work. Over time, further opportunities will present themselves: a change of address or new website; winning an award or competition; inclusion in the latest industry annual; a fresh promotional piece; or even a sample from a glut of printer's proofs. A publishing client once presented me with a pile of spare dust jackets, which I sent out as reminders to commissioners who had liked the illustrator's work. It cost me very little in postage and, within a few days, yielded a lucrative job.

Industry events provide opportunities to meet up with your contacts. They are also a good way to stay in touch with friends and contemporaries who, in turn, might introduce you to some of their contacts or provide you with useful leads. This is networking at its most painless, as all it requires is a genuine interest in your discipline and those who work within it.

'Websites can be created so easily there isn't really any excuse for an illustrator not to have one – the simpler the better… With the invention of the Internet there aren't any boundaries any more.'

Dave Day, Art Director, Fallon

Websites

An online presence is recommended for all practitioners, regardless of their area of expertise, as accessing a website is a quick and easy way for commissioners and employers to check back on work they may have seen some time ago. A personal website is, of course, mandatory for anyone who specializes in web design. How to negotiate the site should be self-evident, and images should be viewable at a generous size and load quickly. The site should be tested and viewable on the browsers most likely to be used by your contacts and type should be legible and free of any typos or spelling errors. While it's unlikely that creative employers lack Flash or are still on dial-up, you may want to have an HTML version, just in case.

If the thought of designing and building your own website terrifies you, approaching a web design student through a local art college could be a cost-effective and mutually beneficial solution. Failing that, some online hosting companies and specialist software manufacturers provide anyone with little or no experience of designing websites with the means to build one from scratch. In addition, a number of professional bodies and sourcebook publishers enable practitioners to upload images to self-maintained online portfolios on a subscription basis. There are also free or cheap image hosting sites, such as Flickr or Photobucket, which allow users to upload and organize limitless images of their work. These boast numerous groups dedicated to design and illustration, and viewers can be linked to individual websites, blogs and/or profiles on MySpace or Facebook. Individual and industry-related blogs, and the online communities that grow up around them, provide further opportunities to promote your work. And there are, of course, numerous web resources, such as Blogger, LiveJournal and WordPress, that enable anyone to start their own blog for free.

'The best thing I did online was buy a simple WISIWIG software package and build my own online portfolio. Much easier for talking to clients; just send a link. Plus it makes you look organized, professional and contemporary. This was not difficult to do and worth it.'

Martin Vintner-Jackson, freelance branding consultant

print & pattern

fabric wallpaper cards gift wrap stationery ceramics

Emma Bridgewater

VOLKSFADEN

custom made super stitched

19 FEBRUARY 2010

DESIGNS...........

BONBI FOREST
ARTWORK & TREATS

hunkydory home
OH! I DO
LIKE TO BE
BESIDE
THE
SEASIDE
...something a bit different!

caroline gardner

for fabric addicts
FABRIC REHAB

Hello Lucky
HELLOLUCKY.CO.UK

when i started print & pattern way back in march 2007 i was very keen
not to use my real name. with the artist banksy in mind i wanted to
operate undercover, especially as i snooped around stores with my little
spy camera looking for fab examples of design. so i adopted 'bowie style'
as a username after a book on my hero david bowie, and have used this
as a pen name ever since. that is until i came to a produce a book, and i
found out that through copyright laws i would need to add my real name
to protect my rights and those of all the contributors. so in the hardest
post i have ever had to write i have to finally reveal a bit about myself.
not easy for me. my name is marie perkins and for the last two years i've
been designing under the studio name 'inkjet designs'. what began as a
fun side project to own an etsy shop soon led to me leaving my textile
design job in order to go freelance.

i did an interview with the british newspaper 'the independent on
sunday' last week and i was worried they would use my real name before
i had a chance to tell you in person - hence im doing it today. we will
have a double page spread in their magazine this sunday and they are
picking images from the book themselves so im not sure which designs
they'll choose. thanks for reading :) here are some little examples of my
own work....

PRINT & PATTERN BOOK ONE

PRINT & PATTERN BOOK TWO

Case study
Print & Pattern blog
Bowie Style

Opposite and below: Marie emerges from anonymity on her blog prior to the publication of the first volume of *Print & Pattern* and showcases some of her own commissions for clients such as Paperchase, Soul UK and Robert Kaufman Fabrics.

Having a blog led UK-based surface-pattern designer, Marie Perkins to a publishing deal. Discovered by Helen Rochester, a senior commissioning editor at Laurence King, the Print & Pattern blog was created by Perkins in 2006. Better known to her readership as Bowie Style, she created Print & Pattern partly because she wanted to highlight this rarely publicized area of design, but also because she had yet to find a blog outside of the US that even acknowledged it. Focusing primarily on decorative design for textiles, tableware, cards and giftwrap, the blog was a natural extension of the mood boards Marie routinely created for the studio she worked for prior to going freelance. Since she'd always enjoyed curating collections of images, Marie jumped at the chance to create the first sourcebook of its kind for Laurence King. The first *Print & Pattern* book was commissioned two years after starting the blog and, such is its success, it is now into its third volume.

In addition to the Print & Pattern blog, which continues to showcase the work of surface pattern designers worldwide, Marie also uses the internet to promote her own work. She has a portfolio website and accompanying blog, on which she posts updates about her commissions. She also has a Flickr archive which links to her Etsy store, where (when deadlines permit) she sells limited edition prints and small giftware items. Since Etsy and its UK-based equivalent, Folksy, are trawled by buyers and commissioners, Marie recommends becoming part of a larger creative community to boost sales and increase web presence. Although the blog and the books can limit the amount of time she is able to spend on her own designs, Marie is happy, despite the late nights they sometimes incur. Design and research are equal passions so the balance is ideal overall.

'I look at a lot of design and art blogs every morning and bookmark them like an online scrapbook. I also look at agents' sites.'

Steve Rutterford, Art Director, Brooklyn Brothers

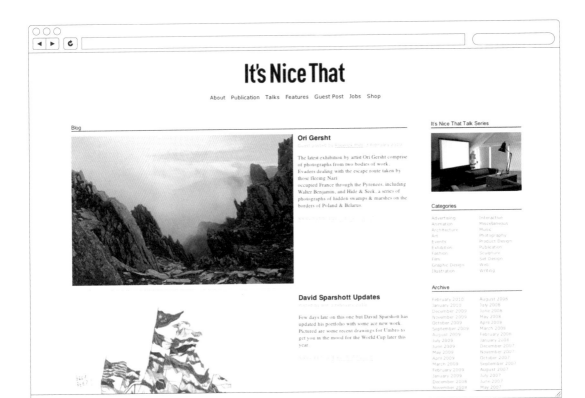

Opposite: Industry-related blogs provide further opportunities to promote your work. It's Nice That is one such blog, focusing on publicizing, promoting and archiving a wide range of work across the creative industry. There are also printed publications (bottom) featuring the best of the work featured on the blog in the six months prior, including interviews with and features written by, current practitioners.

Below: Two graphic design students took the performance route to promoting themselves in the form of a project entitled Keep Us Busy. Creating a shop window studio, they worked inside it for five days on creative projects submitted to them by email. They also documented their progress on a blog.

Sourcebook advertising

Advertising in sourcebooks is another way to keep your work uppermost in the minds of creative employers. Traditionally, this can be cripplingly expensive, but in recent years some publishers have started to produce directories that are specifically aimed at newcomers, and which have considerably cheaper advertising rates. Even publications aimed at established professionals sometimes reduce their rates if a potential advertiser hesitates for long enough, especially if they aren't selling as much advertising space as they had hoped or expected. A friend of mine who prevaricated about taking a double-page advertisement in a well-established illustration directory was eventually offered the spread for the same price as the single page he'd been adamant was all his budget would stretch to.

'I have a long list of bookmarked URL's plus a contact list of over 300 established illustrators. I tend to spend time every couple of months just sorting through the samples I have received, either on spec or updating and managing my bookmarks. And sorting through samples from agencies too.'

Alison Lawn, Art Director, *New Scientist*

Follow-up visits

Although follow-up visits to creative employers who express interest in your work are vital to maintaining professional relationships, it's important that contacts don't feel you are harassing them. If and when someone suggests you keep in touch, ask them when it would be acceptable to contact them again. The answers I've received to this question have varied wildly, from 'Call me at the end of next week' to 'This time next year ought to do it'. Make a note in your diary and do as they ask – even if a promised job didn't happen. There could be any number of reasons why it didn't, and the chances are none of them had anything to do with you.

The majority of your contacts see many portfolios during the course of their working lives. Consequently, they're unlikely to remember every sample that was in yours the last time you showed it to them. Indeed, they might not even have noticed a piece they rave about when you make a follow-up visit, simply because it wasn't relevant to their needs or workload at the time. It's therefore not necessary to replace every sample in your portfolio before you see them again. However, I would advocate following any specific recommendations they may have made, such as losing or improving upon certain pieces – or approaching them again once you have some published work or more experience. Anything you can do to strengthen your portfolio in the interim, including self-set projects with specific employers in mind, can only improve it. Hopefully, world domination won't be far behind.

'I attach PDFs or JPGs to emails to send to a small list of clients and friends. I don't purchase lists. In the past I kept a mailing list of about 1,200 names that received announcements of my exhibitions and lectures.'

Lance Hidy, freelance designer

Summary
Making Yourself
Known in the Marketplace

1.

A face-to-face meeting with a potential employer is a first step towards making yourself known in the creative marketplace; even if they don't have a suitable job or commission, they may recommend you to someone how has – and you will have started to make connections in the industry.

2.

Sending a letter is the best way to make a speculative approach to a company or individual. Designers should include a CV that expands on the information in their letter, while illustrators should send representative samples of their work.

3.

Promotional samples can be used to introduce your work or remind contacts of it after a presentation. Be selective: a single piece of all-purpose material and one or two well-presented samples of your work will have more effect than the entire contents of your portfolio.

4.

Speculative presentations are usually informal, so wear clothes that are smart, comfortable – and add to your self-confidence. A meeting with a client in the financial sector, for example, would require you to dress more formally.

5.

Make sure you arrive at presentations on time, make eye contact with your interviewer/s and show you are familiar with their work. Be prepared for any requests the interviewer may make or problems that may arise – for example, take your mobile phone in case you are delayed.

6.

It is important to keep your work uppermost in the minds of creative employers. Reminders include sending a thank-you note after a presentation, an easily accessible personal website, advertising in sourcebooks and follow-up visits.

Resources

Professional Bodies and Membership Organizations

United Kingdom and Ireland

Design
Chartered Society of Designers
1 Cedar Court
Royal Oak Yard
Bermondsey Street
London SE1 3GA, UK
Tel: +44 20 7357 8088
Email: csd@csd.org.uk
www.csd.org.uk

D&AD
Britannia House
68-80 Hanbury Street
London E1 5JL
Tel: +44 20 7840 1111
Contact via website
www.dandad.org

Design Council
Angel Building
407 St John Street
London EC1V 4AB
Tel: +44 20 7420 5200
Fax: +44 20 7420 5300
www.designcouncil.org.uk

Institute of Designers in Ireland
FX2 the Fumbally Exchange
Fumbally Square
Dublin 8, Ireland
info@idi-design.ie
www.idi-design.ie

Illustration
Association of Illustrators
Somerset House
The Strand
London WC2R 1LA
Tel: +44 20 7759 1010
Email: info@theaoi.com
www.theaoi.com

Illustrators Guild of Ireland
Email:membership@
illustratorsireland.com
www.illustratorsireland.com

North America and Canada

Design
AIGA, the professional
association for design
164 Fifth Avenue
New York, NY 10010, USA
Tel: +1 212 807 1990
www.aiga.org

The Art Directors Club
106 West 29th Street
New York, NY 10001, USA
Tel: +1 212 643 1440
Fax: +1 212 643 4266
Email: info@adcglobal.org
www.adcglobal.org

Organization of Black Designers
300 M Street, SW Suite N-110
Washington, DC 20024–4019, USA
Tel: +1 202 659 3918
Email: info@obd.org
www.obd.org

Société des designers
graphiques du Québec
7255 Rue Alexandra,
Bureau 106 Montréal
Québec H2R 2Y9
Tel: +1 514 842-3960
Fax: +1 514 842-4886
Email: infodesign@sdgq.ca
www. sdgq.ca

Society of Graphic
Designers of Canada
Arts Court, 2 Daly Avenue
Ottawa, Ontario K1N 6E2, Canada
Tel: Toll Free (local) 877 496 4453
Tel: +1 613 567 5400
Email: info@gdc.net
www.gdc.net

Type Directors Club
347 West 36th Street, Suite 603
New York, NY 10018, USA
Tel: +1 212 633 8943
Fax: +1 212 633 8944
Email: director@tdc.org
www.tdc.org

Illustration
Graphic Artists Guild
32 Broadway, Suite 1114
New York, NY 10004, USA
Tel: +1 212 791 3400
Fax: +1 212 791 0333
Email: membership@gag.org
www.gag.org

Illustrator's Partnership of America
845 Moraine Street
Marshfield, MA 02050, USA
Tel: +1 781 837 9152
Email: info@illustratorspartnership.org
www.illustratorspartnership.org

The Society of Illustrators
128 East 63rd Street (between Park
and Lexington Avenues)
New York, NY 10065, USA
Tel: +1 212 838 2560
Fax: +1 212 838 2561
www.societyillustrators.org

Europe

Design
Allianz Deutscher Designer e.V
Steinstrasse 3
38100 Braunschweig, Germany
Tel: +49 53 11 6757
Fax: +49 53 11 6989
Email: info@agd.de
www.agd.de

Art Directors Club Europe
Plaça deis Angels 5 – 6
0800 Barcelona, Spain
Tel: +34 93 44 375 20
Fax: +34 93 32 960 79
Email: office@adceurope.org
www.adceurope.org

Association Typographique
Internationale
c/o Global Meeting Services
10914 Glenda Ct., San Diego
CA 92126, USA
Contact via website
www.atypi.org

Bund Deutscher Grafik-Designer
Warschauer Strasse 59a
Berlin, 10243, Germany
Tel: +49 30 24 53 1490
Fax: +49 30 53 67 0526
Email: info@bdg-designer.de
www.bdg-designer.de

BNO (Association
of Dutch Designers)
Danzigerkade 8a
1013 AP Amsterdam
Pootbus 20698
1001 NR, The Netherlands
Tel: +31 20 624 4748
Fax: +31 20 627 8585
Email: bno@bno.nl
www.bno.nl

Design Austria
im designforum
MuseumsQuartier
Museumsplatz 1/Hof 7
1070 Vienna
A-1070 Austria
Tel: +43 1 524 49 490
Fax: +43 1 524 49 494
Email: info@designaustria.at
www.designaustria.at

Greek Graphic Design Organization
Myllerou 19, Athens, 10436, Greece
Tel: +30 210 522 4813
Email: info@gda.gr
www.gda.gr

Spanish Association
of Design Professionals
Rafael Calvo, 28, Bajo
Madrid, 28010, Spain

Tel: +34 91 319 5589
Fax: +34 91 310 3065
Email: info@aepd.es
www.aepd.es

Swiss Graphic Designers
Bahnhofstrasse 11
Postfach 157
Flawil, 9230, Switzerland
Tel: +41 71 393 4535
Fax: +41 71 393 4548
Email: info@sgd.ch
www.sgd.ch

Union des Designers en Belgique
5 Hof ter Vleesdreef /Box 7
1070 Brussels
Tel: +32 2 523 52 04
Fax: +32 2 558 97 30
Email: welcome@udb.org
www.@udb.org

Illustration
Associazione Illustratori
Via Evangelista Torricelli, 18
20136, Milan, Italy
Tel/Fax: 39 2 3655 3719
Email: info@associazioneillustratori.it
www.associazioneillustratori.it

Associació Professional de
Ilustradores de Catalunya
c/Balmes, 177, 1er. 2ª
08006 Barcelona, Spain
Tel: +34 93 416 1474
Fax: +34 96 415 1583
Email: info@apic.es
www.apic.es

Asociación Profesional de
Ilustradores Euskadi
Andra Maria Kalea
Santa María 3, 1º B –
48005 Bilbao, Spain
Tel: +34 94 675 0885
Email: info@ euskalirudigileak.com
www.euskalirudigileak.com

Associació Professional
d'Illustradors de València
c/ Pintor Martínez Cubells
6 -1r - 1a
46002 – València, Spain
Tel/Fax +34 96 391 3854
www.apiv.es

Asociación Galega de
Profesionais da Illustraciòn
Apartado de Correos 799
C. P. 15001, A Coruña, Spain
Tel: +34 98 190 8874
www.agpi.es

Autillus
c/o Schweizerisches Institut für
Kinder und Jugendmedien
Zeltweg 11

8032 Zürich, Switzerland
Tel: +41 43 268 3900
Fax: +41 43 268 3909
Email: info@sikjm.ch
www.autillus.ch

Federación de Asociaciones
de Ilustradores Profesionales
de Madrid
Calle Mayor 4,
Planta 4a, Oficina 6
28013 Madrid, Spain
Tel: +34 91 531 8670
Email: info@fadip.org
www.fadip.org

Illustratoren Organization e.V.
Mergenthalerstraße 4
60388 Frankfurt am Main, Germany
Tel: +49 69 36 70 4859
Fax: +49 69 36 70 4860
www.illustratoren-organization.de

La Maison des Illustrateurs
127 rue du Chevaleret
75013 Paris, France
Tel: +33 1 44 24 0889
Fax: +33 1 56 61 1702
Email: maisonillustr@free.fr
www.lamaisondesillustrateurs.com

Vlaamse Illustratoren
Lange Leemstraat 264
2018 Antwerp, Belgium
Email: info@vlaamse-illustratoren.com
www.flemish-illustrators.com

Scandinavia

Design
FÍT Association of Icelandic
Graphic Designers
PO Box 590
121 Reykjavik
Iceland
Tel: +354 771 2200
Email: fit@teiknarar.is
www.teiknarar.is

Grafia
Uudenmaankatu 11 B 9
Helsinki, FIN-00120, Finland
Tel: +358 9 601 942
Email: grafia@grafia.fi
www.grafia.fi

Sveriges Designer
Box 7477
103 92 Stockholm, Sweden
Email: info@sverigesdesigner.se
www.sverigesdesigner.se

Illustration
Grafill
Rosenkrantz Gate 21,
0160 Oslo, Norway
Tel: +47 22 12 82 00

Email: grafill@grafill.no
www.grafill.no

Illustratörcentrum
Årstaängsvägen 1C, 7tr
117 43 Stockholm, Sweden
Tel: +46 8 642 3792
Email: info@illustratorcentrum.se
www.illustratorcentrum.se

Kuvittajat
Albertinkatu 1
00150 Helsinki
Email: info@kuvittajat.fi
www.kuvittajat.fi

Svenska Technare
Arstaängsvägen 5B
S-117 43 Stockholm, Sweden
Tel: +46 8 556 02 910
Fax: +46 8 556 02 919
Email: info@svenskatecknare.se
www.svenskatecknare.se

Australia and New Zealand

Design
Australian Graphic Design
Association
PO Box 816
Unley, SA 5061, Australia
Tel: +61 8 8410 9228
Fax: +61 8 8410 9229
Email: secretariat@agda.com.au
www.agda.com.au

Design Institute of Australia
GPO Box 355
Melbourne, Victoria 3001
Australia http://sphotos-e.ak.fbcdn.
net/hphotos-ak-ash3/545190_101
51082202837953_619641424_n.
jpg
Tel: +61 3 966 22 345
Fax: +61 3 966 24 140
Email: admin@design.org.au
www.design.org.au

Design Institute of New Zealand
PO Box 109423
Auckland, New Zealand
Tel: +64 9 529 1713
Fax: +64 9 529 1714
Email: designer@dinz.org.nz
www.dinz.org.nz

Illustration
Illustrators Australia
Abbotsford Convent
Convent Building, C1.22
1 St Heliers Street
Abbotsford, Victoria
Australia 3067
Tel: +61 3 941 91 355
Email: office@illustratorsaustralia.com
www.illustratorsaustralia.com

Information and Advice

Professional Portfolio Advice

Association of Illustrators
(see page 136 for contact details).
www.theaoi.com

BNO (Association of Dutch
Designers)
(see page 136 for contact details).
www.bno.nl

Chartered Society of Designers
(see page 136 for contact details).
www.csd.org.uk

The One Club
(see page 140 for contact details).
www.oneclub.org

Museums and Libraries

St Bride Library
Bride Lane, Fleet Street
London EC4Y 8EE, UK
Tel: +44 20 7353 4660
Fax: +44 20 7583 7073
www.stbride.org

M.A.X Museo
Via Dante Alighieri 6
CH-6830 Chiasso
Switzerland
Tel: +41 91 682 56 56
Fax: +41 91 682 56 65
Email: info@maxmuseo.ch
www.maxmuseo.ch

Museum of American Illustration
The Society of Illustrators
128 East 63rd Street (between
Park and Lexington Avenues)
New York, NY 10065, USA
Tel: +1 212 838 2560
Fax: +1 212 838 2561
Email: info@societyofillustrators.org
www.societyillustrators.org

The Type Museum
100 Hackford Road
London SW19 0QU, UK
Tel: +44 20 7735 0055
Email: enquiries@typemuseum.org
www.typemuseum.org

Portfolio Manufacturers and Suppliers

Standard Commercial

Blick Art Materials
P.O. Box 1267
Galesburg
IL 61402-1267, USA
Tel: +1 800 828 4548
Fax: +1 800 621 8293
www.dickblick.com

London Graphics Centre
Covent Garden Flagship Store
16–18 Shelton Street
London WC2H 9JL, UK
Tel: +44 20 7759 4500
Fax: +44 20 7759 4585
www.londongraphics.co.uk

Paperhaus
8406A Beverly Boulevard
Los Angeles, CA 90048
USA
Email: info@paperhaus.com
www.paperhaus.com

Portfolios-and-Art-Cases.com
4938 Hampden Lane, Suite 345
Bethesda, MD 20814, USA
Tel: +1 301 654 7055
Fax: +1 301 654 7056
Email: sales@portfolios-and-art-
cases.com
www.portfolios-and-art-cases.com

Tailor-made/Handmade

Archival Methods
230-2 Middle Road
Henrietta, NY 14467, USA
Tel: +1 585 334 7050
Fax: +1 585 334 7067
Email: mail@archivalmethods.com
www.archivalmethods.com

Brodies
17 Shorts Gardens,
Unit 3, 2nd Floor,
London WC2H 9AT
Tel: +44 20 7379 5755
Email: brodie@brodiesportfolios.com
www.brodiesportfolios.com

Wyvern Bindery
56–58 Clerkenwell Road
London EC1M 5PX, UK
Tel. +44 20 7490 7899
info@wyvernbindery.com
www.wyvernbindery.com

Useful Design Websites

Blogs and Communities

www.designers-who-blog.com
Includes links to blogs by graphic and web designers, illustrators, typographers, logo designers, branders and more.

www.artyears.com
Site devoted to print, web and typographic design, illustration and photography; it offers articles, reviews, tutorials and the opportunity to showcase work.

www.commarts.com
The website of Communication Arts magazine offers a plethora of industry news plus information about jobs and competitions.

www.dandad.org
D&AD blog.

www.designersarewankers.com
Houses plebsville, a community dedicated to communicating with other creative individuals, to help up-and-coming designers understand the industry. Boasts an 'online human search engine' who provides impartial guidance and act as a gateway to industry leaders willing to provide advice.

www.designiskinky.com
Australian blog featuring design and job news.

www.dexigner.com
Design-related news, events, competitions and resources; also provides a design directory, database, agenda and weekly newsletter.

www.logodesignlove.com
Logo appreciation site featuring articles and resources for designers.

Online Website Builders

www.bigblackbag.com
www.foliosnap.com
www.homestead.com
www.moonfruit.com
www.one.com

Self-promotion

www.altpick.com
Online, self-managed portfolio site for graphic, web and interactive designers as well as illustrators, photographers and animators.

www.cargocollective.com
Invitation-only outfit offering a free basic promotional website or a paid freestanding one with its own url. Allows members to build a personal network to follow and comment on the work of others in the community. Frequently awards unaffiliated talent with membership on sharing samples of their work.

www.coroflot.com
Designer-run portfolio site covering a wide variety of creative disciplines. Membership is free and the site also offers an extensive job board and employer directory.

www.creativeshake.com
Online resource that showcases creative talent; also features a job board. Advertisers include graphic designers, art directors, creative directors and illustrators.

www.flavors.me
Site enabling creative practitioners to centralize all their online accounts. Automatically organizes content from 35 services into an elegant and cohesive online presence. Basic free service available.

www.figdig.com
Community dedicated to allowing creative professionals to upload, manage and showcase their work online for free. Membership includes illustrators and designers working in many disciplines and media.

www.guru.com
This website's mission is to provide businesses with the most efficient platform to connect, and perform transactions, with freelance professionals locally, nationally and globally.

www.voodoochilli.net
Free online resource and portfolio service for visual artists and clients looking for talent. Covers a wide variety of disciplines including graphic design, web design, product design and illustration.

Useful Illustration Websites

Blogs and Communities

www.theaoi.com
Association of Illustrators website; resources for commissioners and practitioners.

www.concretehermitnetwork.com
Networking site that encourages members to share, discuss and promote their work, blog and join groups of like-minded artists. Affiliated with the gallery and publisher of the same name and links to forthcoming events.

www.drawger.com
Blogs for and by illustrators, by invitation only. Includes chat forums and a non-juried annual online exhibit, to which members submit their favourite work.

www.drawn.ca
Multi-author illustration blog containing links and resources.

www.escapefromillustrationisland.com
Resources and inspiration for illustrators, featuring tutorials, podcasts, articles, bookstore, and numerous links to illustration-centric communities, organizations and business advice blogs.

www.illustrationage.com
Illustration news portal showcasing work by the international illustration community.

www.illustrationfriday.com
Sets a weekly illustration challenge and allows illustrators to comment and give critical feedback.

www.illustrationmundo.com
Provides a central location where professional and aspiring illustrators can showcase their work, be inspired, share information and seek advice.

www.thelittlechimpsociety.com
Illustration news portal.

www.scamp.ie
Blog by members and associates of the Illustrators Guild of Ireland.

Self-promotion

www.aoiportfolios.com
Portfolios are managed by the individual artists; the website is open to all, with reduced fees offered to members of the Association of Illustrators.

www.behance.net
Platform for creative professionals to showcase their work online for free; also promotes competitions, links to professional organizations and blogs, offers professional tips, and advertises jobs.

www.contact-creative.com
Online portfolios hosted by the publisher of Contact Illustrators (see Illustration Directories for contact details). Illustrators not wishing to take out advertising in the directory can showcase their work online.

www.theispot.com
Showcases the work of illustrators from over 15 countries and serves buyers throughout the world; also handles stock illustration and facilitates talk with fellow illustrators.

www.figdig.com
Online community for illustrators and designers.

www.flavors.me
Site enabling creative practitioners to centralize all their online accounts Organizes content from 35 services into a cohesive online presence. Basic free service available.

www.hireanillustrator.com
Portfolio website and promotional service affiliated with the Little Chimp Society.

www.illoz.com
Invitation-only portfolio site. Also functions as a space that art directors can use to commission a job and follow it through. Illustrators pay for the service; art directors get it for free but have to apply for an account or be referred by another art director.

www.folioplanet.com
Directory of illustrator links, online portfolios and stock illustration images.

Useful
Publications

Design Magazines

Applied Arts
18 Wynford Drive, Suite 411
Toronto, Ontario M3C 3S2
Canada
Tel: +1 800 646 0347
Fax: +1 416 510 0913
www.appliedartsmag.com

Baseline: International
TypoGraphics Magazine
Bradbourne Publishing Limited
Bradbourne House
East Malling
Kent ME19 6DZ, UK
Tel: +44 1732 875200
Fax: +44 1732 875300
www.baselinemagazine.com

Communication Arts
110 Constitution Drive,
Menlo Park, CA 94025, USA
Tel: +1 650 326 6040,
Fax: +1 650 326 1648
www.commarts.com

Creative Review
79 Wells Street
London W1T 3QN
UK
Tel: +44 20 7970 4000
www.creativereview.com

Design Edge Canada
North Island Publishing Ltd
8–1606 Sedlescomb Drive
Mississauga, Ontario L4X 1M6
Canada
Tel: +1 905 625 7070
Fax: +1 905 625 4856
www.designedgecanada.com

Design Week
Centaur Media PLC
(see Creative Review)
www.designweek.co.uk

Desktop
Niche Media
170 Dorcas Street
South Melbourne,
Victoria 3205, Australia
Tel: +61 3 9948 4900
www.desktopmag.au

DZone
Three Publishers BV
Binnenkadijk 329
1018 AX Amsterdam, Holland
Tel: +32 20 625 6782
Email: info@threepublishers.com
www.dzone.nl

Graphic Design USA
89 Fifth Avenue, Suite 901
New York, New York 10003, USA
Tel: +1 212 696 4380
Fax: +1 212 696 4564
www.gdusa.com

HOW
PO Box 421751
Palm Coast, FL 32142-1751 USA
Tel: +1 386 246 3365
www.howdesign.com

IDPure
Chemin du Pré 4A, Case postale
1110 Morges 1, Switzerland
Tel: +41 21 802 50 84
Fax: +41 21 802 50 76
Email: info@idpure.com
www.idpure.com

Items
De Wittenstraat 102-104
1052 BB Amsterdam
Postbus 10189
1001 ED Amsterdam Holland
Tel: +31 20 682 9479
Email: info@items.nl.

Print
38 East 29th Street, 3rd Floor
New York, NY 10016, USA
Tel: +1 212 447 1400
Fax: +1 212 447 5231
www.printmag.com

Design Directories

Black Book Creative
Industry Directory
740 Broadway, Suite 202
New York, NY 10003, USA
Tel: +1 212 979 6700
Email: eryder@blackbook.com
www.blackbook.com

Creative Handbook
Centaur Media PLC,
50 Poland Street
London W1F 7AX, UK
Tel: +44 20 7970 4000
www.chb.com

Creative Match
www.creativematch.co.uk

Le Book London
43–44 Hoxton Square
London N1 6BP, UK
Tel: +44 20 7739 1155
Fax: +44 20 7739 1188

Le Book Paris
4 rue d'Enghien
75010 Paris, France
Tel: +33 1 47 70 03 30
Fax: +33 1 48 24 04 84

Le Book New York
552 Broadway, 6th Floor
New York, NY 10012, USA
Email: info@lebook.com
www.lebook.com

Further Reading

Auteursrecht voor ontwerpers
(Association of Dutch Designers)
Published by the BNO (see
page 136 for contact details).
www.bno.nl

Graphic Artists Guild Handbook:
Pricing and Ethical Guidelines
Published by the Graphic Artists
Guild (see page 136 for details).
www.gag.org

Handboek Voor Het Opzetten Van
Een Ontwerppraktijk
(Handbook For Starting Your
Own Creative Company)
By V. van den Eijnde, K. de Jong
and M. van Leest
BIS Publishers Het Sieraad
Postjesweg 1, 1057 DT Amsterdam
The Netherlands
Tel: +31 20 515 0230
Fax: +31 20 515 0239
Email: bis@bispublishers.nl

How To Be A Graphic Designer
Without Losing Your Soul
By Adrian Shaughnessy
Laurence King Publishing Ltd
361–373 City Road
London EC1V 1LR, UK
Tel: +44 20 7841 6900
Fax: +44 20 7841 6910
Email: info@laurenceking.com
www.laurenceking.com

Illustration Magazines

3 x 3 Magazine
Published by Charles Hively
244 Fifth Avenue, Suite F269
New York, NY 10001, USA
Tel: +1 212 591 2566
Fax: +1 212 537 6201
Email: chively@3x3mag.com
www.3x3mag.com

Artists & Illustrators
The Chelsea Magazine Company
Liscartan House,
127-131 Sloane Street,
London,
SW1X 9ASUK
Tel: + 44 20 7901 8000
Fax: + 44 20 7901 8001
info@chelseamagazines.com
www.artistsandillustrators.co.uk

Black Book Illustration
740 Broadway, Suite 202
New York, NY 10003, USA
Tel: +1 212 979 6700
Email: eryder@blackbook.com
www.blackbook.com

Communication Arts
110 Constitution Drive,
Menlo Park, CA 94025, USA
Tel: +1 650 326 6040,
Fax: +1 650 326 1648
www.commarts.com

Illustration Directories

Directory of Illustration
Published by Serbin Communications
813 Reddick Street
Santa Barbara, CA 93101, USA
Tel: +1 805 963 0439/800 876 6425
Fax: +1 805 965 0496
Email: admin@serbin.com
www.directoryofillustration.com

Contact Illustration
Contact Creative UK LLP
PO Box 397
Reigate Surrey RH2 2ES
Tel: 01731 241 399
Email contact via website
www.contact-creative.com

Ilustration Magazine
39 Elmsleigh Road
Twickenham Middlesex TW2 5EF
www.illustration-mag.com

Varoom
Published by the Association of
Illustrators (see page 136 for
contact details).

Further Reading

How To Be an Illustrator
By Darrel Rees
Laurence King Publishing Ltd
361–373 City Road
London EC1V 1LR, UK
Tel: +44 20 7841 6900
Fax: +44 20 7841 6910
Email: info@laurenceking.com
www.laurenceking.com

The Illustrators Guide to Law
and Business Practice
Published by the Association of
Illustrators.

Index

Picture Credits

The author and publisher would like to thank the following for providing images for use in this book. In all cases, every effort has been made to credit the copyright holders, but should there be any omissions or errors the publisher would be pleased to insert the appropriate acknowledgement in any subsequent edition (t=top, b=bottom, l=left, r=right, m=middle): P8, 1st row, l: Stuart Briers; 2nd row, r: Prat Fabrication, Prat Pampa Spiral book with polypropylene or polyester sleeves from Prat Paris, www.pratfab.com; 3rd row: Mapac Group Ltd, www.mapac.com; 4th row, l: Acer Inc. www.acer.co.uk; r: Apple Inc, Cupertino, California, USA. P11b and p14-15: Darren Custance online CV; p11t Austin Driscoll concept sketches. P12t: Tonia Ibrahim digital portfolio; p12b: Archival Methods LLC – Presentation supplies, www.archivalmethods.com, 235 Middle Road, Henrietta, NY 14467 USA. P16t: GUP Magazine spread designed by Matthew West of Two.Seventy, www.twoseventy.co.uk, Photography © Henk Wildschut and Raimond Wouda; b: 1920 typeface designed by Matthew West of Two.Seventy. P17t: 33 logo mark and website designed by Matthew West of Two.Seventy; b: Autobob logotype and website designed by Matthew West of Two.Seventy. P20–21: Illustration and typography by Andy Smith www.asmithillustration.com. P24: ebooks from MySkoob, designed by Strichpunkt Design. P26: Moog Acid – Art Direction: Kjell Ekhorn, Jon Forss, Designers: Kjell Ekhorn, Jon Forss, Design firm: Non-Format, Miniature models & photography: Dan McPharlin, Client: Lo Recordings. P28: Vitsoe.com – website design and build by Airside with associates. P29: The Stitches – created by Anne Brassier and Airside. P30: The Grand Tour Website and digital experience: Digit. Project created in association with The Partners, The National Gallery and Hewlett Packard. Art Director: Andrew Dean, Design and Illustration: Michelle Bower, Technical Build: Tony Currie. Photo credits: Bathers at La Grenouillère by Claude-Oscar Monet courtesy of Andrew Dean; The Ambassadors by Hans Holbein the Younger courtesy of Andrew Dean; Samson and Delilah by Peter Paul Reubens courtesy of Fergus Jackson. P31: NewWork Magazine. Editor in Chief/Creative Director/Art Director: Ryotatsu Tanaka, Ryo Kumazaki, Hitomi Ishigaki, Aswin Sadha. Design: Studio NewWork. P32: Balance Advert for The Economist: Art Direction: Paul Cohen, Copywriter: Mark Fairbanks, Illustration: Kjell Ekhorn, Jon Forss, Design firm: Non-Format, Client: AMV BBDO. P33: as for p24. P34: Kick Out Bigotry campaign: Design, Art Direction, Copy Writing: Ed Watt, Design-ed, www.design-ed.co.uk. Campaign Logos: Hookson, www.hookson.com. Copyright: Kick-Out Bigotry and Football For All Logos © Hookson. All other design © Football For All. Campaign Photography: Paul Hampton, two bob rocket, www.twobobrocket.co.uk. Campaign Director: Roddy McNulty, Football For All. P35: Call Centre In A Box: Designer: Nic Shuttleworth, I Like Blue, www.ilikeblue.co.uk. Company: Iris Associates, Client: Voice. P38t: Eniro 118 118 campaign: Illustrations: Erica Jacobson 2008, Ad company: Ogilvy Advertising, AD Richard Baynham, Copy Per-Olof Lundgren. Campaign for Eniro 118 118, a Swedish search company that helps people to find people, business and products. Technique: Gouache, pens and Illustrator. P38b: Bulmers 'Friends of British Summertime' campaign. © Exposure www.exposure.net. On behalf of Bulmers. P37: Boscos Endins Advertising campaign: Illustrator:Adrià Fruitós (www.adfruitos.com), Graphic designer: Josep Bagà, www.josepbaga.com, Client: Dagoll Dagom – theatre company, www.dagolldagom.com/boscosendins. P40: Gulf Air magazine images © Ink Publishing. P41: Rock of Ages cover and Doctor Who feature images courtesy of the Radio Times. P42-43: Design Week web magazine. P44: Snob Magazine, Art Direction: Ilya Baranov. P45t: 'The Science of Music' Utne Reader, November/December 2008, Illustrator: Nate Johannes, Art Director Stephanie Glaros; b: frankie magazine, Morrison Media. Illustration by Sara Hingle for frankie magazine www.frankie.com.au. P46: Illustrations by Michelle Thompson, www.michelle-thompson.com: (t) The Globe & Mail Commissioned by Cinders McLeod; (b) CPO Agenda Commissioned by Redactive Media. P47: b.spirit! and b.there! Magazine spreads images © Ink Publishing. P48: Varoom: Art Direction: Kjell Ekhorn, Jon Forss, Designers: Kjell Ekhorn, Jon Forss, Design firm: Non-Format, Editor: Adrian Shaughnessy, Publisher: Derek Brazell / The Association of Illustrators. P49: The Illustrated Ape magazine, issue 25: Heavenly in association with Heavenly Records. Cover image © Tim Fishlock. P50tl: Natural Flights of the Human Mind – Clare Morrall, Illustrator: Harriet Russell, Art Direction: Alasdair Oliver, Publisher: Hodder; tm: The Truth About These Strange Times – Adam Foulds, Illustrator: Harriet Russell, Art Direction: Steve Marking, Publisher: Orion; tr: Living with the Laird – Belinda Rathbone, Illustrator: Harriet Russell, Art Direction: Julian Humphries, Publisher: HarperCollins; bl: Tout Sweet written by Karen Wheeler, artwork by Andy Robert Davies, www.ardillustration.com, Publisher: Summersdale; bm: Meeting Mr. Kim, Illustrator: Andy Robert Davies, Publisher: Summersdale; br: The Rattle Bag, Edited by Seamus Heaney and Ted Hughes, Illustrator: Nigel Owen (represented by CIA), Publisher: Faber & Faber. P53: Adolie Day, www.adolieday.blogspot.com. Stationery – La Marelle edition, Le Chasseur de papillons – Toucan editions, Lilichou – Amaterra, Nouvel Angle. P54: David Roberts represented by Artist Partners, www.artistpartners.com. Images on behalf of Faber & Faber from Ten Sorry Tales by Mick Jackson, with illustrations by David Roberts, first published by Faber and Faber in 2005 (Isbn 225489). P55: El Oso y el Cuervo, Copyright: Illustrations: André da Loba (www.andredaloba.com/), Text: Monika Klose, First Edition/Publisher: OQO Editora, www.oqo.es, Languages: Spanish, Portuguese, English and French. ISBN-13: 978-8496788596, ISBN-10: 8496788598. Hardcover: 48 pages. P56tl: Homework for Grown-Ups – E.Foley & B.Coates, Cover designed by Liam Relph, Illustration: Christopher Wormell, Published by Square Peg; tm: The Heart Of Success – Rob Parsons, Cover designed by David Wardle, www.designedbydavid.co.uk, Published by Hodder and Stoughton; tr: The Sixty Minute Father – Rob Parsons, Cover designed by David Wardle, www.designedbydavid.co.uk, Published by Hodder and Stoughton; bl: Sag Harbor – Colson Whitehead, Cover designed by Liam Relph, Illustration: Liam Relph, Published by Harvill Secker; bm: Changing Grooms – Sasha Wagstaff, Cover designed by Henry Steadman, www.henrysteadman.com, Cover commissioned and art directed by Claire Bentley, Headline Publishing; br: Florian del Cassonetto – Ornella Della Libera, Client: Rizzoli Italy, Studio:

Mucca Design, Creative Director: Matteo Bologna, Art Director: Erica Heitman-Ford, Design: Meg Paradise www.megparadise.com. P57: The Little Black Book Of Red Tape – Ian Vince. Cover designed by Henry Steadman, Cover commissioned and art directed by Nick May, Orion Publishing. P58: Couture Interiors: Calligraphy: Peter Horridge, Cover design: Eleanor Ridsdal, Photographer: Steven Fisher, Publisher: Laurence King publishing Ltd. P59t: The Bible (Contemporary Edition). Illustrated by Steve Wilson, www.wilson2000.com, Publisher: Hodder and Stoughton, Designer: Mark Read; b: Lincoln – James L. Swanson. Illustrated and designed by Rafael Nobre, Published by Record. P60: Chloe Noonan. Created and designed by Marc Ellerby, www.marcellerby.com. P62: The Double cover by Tom Gauld, Nobrow Ltd. P63tl: The New Ghost cover by Robert Hunter, Nobrow Ltd., p63tr: The Double cover by Gwenola Carerre, Nobrow Ltd; P63b: The New Ghost by Robert Hunter, Nobrow Ltd. P64: All images from Elephantmen comic and associated projects. Images by Boo Cook. Published by Active Images via Active Comics. P65: Three Incestuous Sisters – Audrey Niffenegger. Reprinted by permission of The Random House Group Ltd. P67: Bahn TV Idents. Art Direction, Design, Animation: Sascha Vernwiebe, www.saschaverwiebe.com. Client: Deutsche Bahn AG, Production Company: Atkon AG. P68: Ladyhawke, My Delirium, video directed by Frater, www.fraterfilms.com. Illustrations by Sarah Larnach. Courtesy of Modular Recordings. P70: Storyboard by Graham Humphreys for director Eitan Arrusi's feature film Reverb. P71: Flick (2008), artwork by Alex Tomlinson www.alex-tomlinson.com. Copyright Alex Tomlinson, courtesy of Monster Films. P73: Wallace and Gromit: Invention Suspension. Game images by Aardman Digital, Aardman Animations Ltd. P74: Machinarium, Amanita Design, www.amanita-design.net. Design, Director: Jakub Dvorsky, Animation: Vaclav Blin. Jaromir Plachy, Programming: David Oliva, Graphics: Adolf Lachman, Jakub Pozar, Music: Tomas Dvorak (Floex), Sound : Tomas Dvorak (Pif). P75: Character design and development by Anna Zukowska. Student at Staffordshire University, Msc 3D Games Modelling. Lecturer Alex Jackson. From top left: Character base mesh screengrab from Zbrush. Zbrush software © Pixologic Inc. Bottom left: Rendered image from Zbrush with 'MatCap' material applied. ZBrush software © Pixologic Inc. P76 tl-tr: Toika and Arctic Breakers, Card Designs. Images and Copyright by Andrew Pavitt, www.andrewpavitt.com; b: Electro Birthday, Artwork created by Rachel Harper, www.rahrahrepeats.blogspot.com. Artwork created to license through Inspire by Design Ltd. www.inspirebydesign.org. P78: Siobhan Harrison, www.siobhanharrison.co.uk; l: Get Well card for Images and Editions; r: Floral Mother's Day card for Rainbow. P80 and 131: Alix Jeambrum. P84-85: Tien-Min Liao. P86: David Arias self promotional and portfolio book © David Arias, www.arias.ca. P87: © Russell Cobb. P89: Creative Review. Illustration: Billie Jean, www.billiejean.co.uk. Art Direction: Nathan Gale, Editor: Patrick Burgoyne. P90tl: AIGA, the professional association for design www.aiga.org; tr: The Design Council, www.designcouncil.org.uk; bl: Courtesy of the D&AD, www.dandad.org; br: Society Of Illustrators Inc. www.societyillustrators.org. Normal Rockwell header image © SEPS 1935. P94: Michael Redmond for V&A competition. P96: Matt Bolton. P102: Rob Moxon Portfolio, www.robmoxon.co.uk. Work produced whilst studying at the University of Cumbria. Type Factory Museum (ISTD Student Brief 2009). We Love Graphic Design, Fanzine – Robert Moxon, Sofia Frykler and Dan Tucker. P104: Shaun Doyle Illustration. Images © Shaun Doyle, www.shaundoyle.co.uk. P106t: Shaun Doyle Illustration. Images © Shaun Doyle; b: Images ©Russell Cobb. P108: Layout for website, www.janinerewell.com © Janine Rewell. Dancing With The Dead and Dollhouse images © Janine Rewell. P110: Portfolio provided by Lydia Fee, www.lydiafee.co.uk, hello@lydiafee.co.uk. P114: Raewyn Brandon. P118: Portfolio provided by Brodies Portfolio and Bag Emporium. Myriad Resources Ltd T/A Brodies, www.brodiesportfolios.com. P119: Portfolio and illustrations by Lydia Fee (see p110). P121-22: Demonstration illustrations created by Jem Robinson, www.jemillo.com. P123t: Images © Stuart Briers; br: Images © Gemma Robinson, www.gemma-robinson.co.uk. Published by Human Resources Magazine, Haymarket Publications. P124: Sam Dallyn Portfolio, www.samdallyn.co.uk. Website Design/Information Architecture: Sam Dallyn, Flash Site Build/XML: Andy Biggs. P126: D&AD New Blood portfolio workshop. P132t: Rob Ryan for Wild & Wolf; p132b: Rob Ryan for Coutts Bank, Agency Coley Porter Bell, for Kids Company charity. P133: Julia Pott, Etsy web page. P134-135: © Sophie Blackall, Missed Connections, Love Lost and Found, Workman 2011. P136-137: Secret Weapon postcards by Linzie Hunter; P138l: Marc and Anna Christmas Tea Towel – designed by Marc & Anna, www.marcandanna.co.uk. P139: Because Studio Folio Book. Images © Loz Ives, Because Studio, www.becausestudio.co.uk. P140: Girls Who Draw; tl: Love to Print box designed by Yee Ting Kuit, www.lovetoprint.blogspot.com; tr: Postcard designed by Gemma Correll from the Love to Print boxset; bl: Misfits book cover designed by Gemma Correll, www.girlswhodraw.wordpress.com; br: Postcard designed by Bogus Baby from the Misfits book. P141tl: Jay Taylor Promotional Books. Images © Jay Taylor, www.scribblejay.co.uk; b: Barnaby Richards 20 Things Books. Images © Barnaby Richards, www.barnabyrichards.co.uk, things@barnabyrichards.com. P144t: Selected Works © Remote Location, www.remote-location.com; m: Caroline Fabes, www.carolinefabes.com. Website designed by Caroline Fabes, thanks to Indexhibit; b: Polly Dunbar. Website Designed by Dave Adcock, www.ten4design.co.uk, Illustrations by Polly Dunbar. Right illustration from SHOE BABY © 2005 Polly Dunbar, Reproduced by permission of Walker Books Ltd, London SE11 5HJ, www.pollydunbar.com, www.walker.co.uk. Images © Polly Dunbar. P146-147: Print & Pattern blog by Bowie Style. P148: It's Nice That - Will Hudson and Alex Bec, www.itsnicethat.com. P149: Thomas Lovell and Shaun Hughes, www.keep-us-busy.com.